HERE BE DRAGONS!

Navigating the Hazards
found in
Canadian Family Research

A Guide for Genealogists

with Some Uncommon Useful Knowledge

by

Althea Douglas, M.A., C.G.(C)

Toronto: The Ontario Genealogical Society, 1996

Further copies of this book and information about the Ontario Genealogical Society can be obtained by writing to:
Suite 102, 40 Orchard View Boulevard,
Toronto, ON, Canada M4R 1B9

ISBN 0-7779-0196-X

Canadian Cataloguing in Publication Data

Douglas, Althea, 1926-
  Here be dragons! : navigating the hazards found in
Canadian family research : a guide for genealogists

Includes bibliographical references.
ISBN 0-7779-0196-X

1. Canada - Genealogy - Handbooks, manuals, etc.
2. Canada - History - Miscellaneous.
I. Ontario Genealogical Society. II. Title,

CS83.D68 1995   929'.1'072071   C95-932632-4

Printed by Print Central

Published by
The Ontario Genealogical Society
Suite 102, 40 Orchard View Boulevard
Toronto, Ontario, Canada M4R 1B9

MULTI PATRIAE
PRIORES • MULTAE

Founded 1961

published with assistance from The Ministry of Citizenship, Culture and Recreation

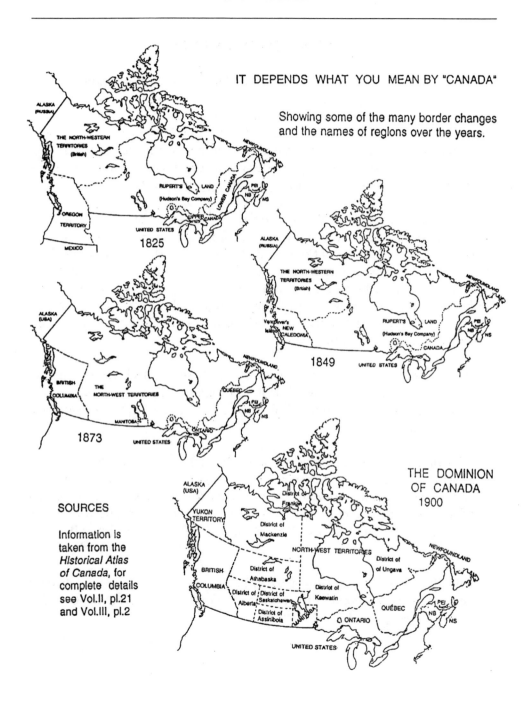

IT DEPENDS WHAT YOU MEAN BY "CANADA"

Showing some of the many border changes and the names of regions over the years.

SOURCES

Information is taken from the *Historical Atlas of Canada,* for complete details see Vol.II, pl.21 and Vol.III, pl.2

THE DOMINION OF CANADA 1900

ACKNOWLEDGEMENTS

My thanks first to Clifford Collier and the Manuscript Advisory Committee of the Ontario Genealogical Society who encouraged my first tentative ideas, accepted the early draft, and then helped to check and polished the final text; in particular, Ruth Burkholder, Brenda Dougall Merriman, and J. Brian Gilchrist, all of whom made valuable comments and suggestions. Jane MacNamara's advice and help in designing the volume has been indispensable. The mistakes that remain are all my own work.

When it came time to find visual examples of some of the puzzles and problems discussed in this booklet, my gratitude goes to my husband's ancestors: James Douglas of Collin and Mouswald parishes in Dumfries-shire, Scotland, who saved letters from home, the ticket for his family's passage to Quebec, his Militia Commission, and a wide variety of leases, receipts, and ephemera; and his son, William James Douglas who, over many decades, kept a brief daily diary that tells us much about a farmer's life, his chores and his travels of over a century ago.

The map used on the cover is courtesy the National Archives of Canada, National Map Collection: detail from Bolognino Zaltieri. *Il Disegno dil discoperto della nova Franza*, 1566. State 2 (NMC-22900). The dragon was drawn by myself.

The Frontispiece maps showing the many border changes and the names of the various regions of Canada were also prepared by myself, based on Plate 21 in Volume II of the *Historical Atlas of Canada* (citation listed on Page 10). Readers wishing more complete details on border changes, and the treaties involving these, should refer to Plate 21 and also Plate 2 in Volume III of the *HAC.*

Finally, the view of the Mirimichi River in New Brunswick, showing its early settlement, is also courtesy of the National Archives of Canada (NAC-C41755).

Althea Douglas
Ottawa, 1996

HERE BE DRAGONS !
Navigating the Hazards found in Canadian Family Research

ILLUSTRATIONS

Chapter 1

INTRODUCTION

Here be Dragons!

One of the first letters I received when I started out as a professional genealogist asked "Where is Upper Canada? My great-grandmother said she was born there but I cannot find it on any map." Most central Canadians know there was once an Upper Canada and a Lower Canada, though they may not be quite sure when these terms were used. To researchers from outside Canada, now-obsolete place names are unfamiliar and our uses of them can be confusing.

As a child in New Brunswick, I learned that "Upper Canadians" were rich industrialists and bankers from Montreal and Toronto who had exploited the Maritimes ever since Confederation. When we moved to Toronto, I found out that not everyone there was rich and that many of the bankers were Maritimers. I also learned that Ontario was once called Upper Canada, then later, Canada West—which was not the same thing as Western Canada, where my uncles lived.

What we now call Canada is filled with similar-sounding place names that often change over the years. Canadian geography commemorates almost every British city, county, famous battle, peer and politician, often in more than one place. In Quebec, along with nobles and notables, there are the Saints, and for those popularly-used ones, some identifying geographic location must be added. Place-name hazards abound, waiting for Canadians as well as researchers from abroad.

There are other shoals lying in wait for unwary voyagers into the past. Leslie P. Hartley, in his "Prologue" to *The Go-Between* (1953) put it briefly:
"The past is a foreign country; they do things differently there."

Genealogists and family historians are time travellers diligently searching the past and, because many things they encounter appear familiar, they are sometimes not aware when a custom, a social attitude, or the way of doing things was really quite different.

Here be Dragons!

This booklet grew out of a series of one-page explanations about such hazards and misunderstandings. The third client who asked about "Upper Canada" received my first "Notes On ..." sheet; next came one on the spelling of names and literacy; then came townships and land divisions; and so it grew.

Like the apocryphal "Here be Dragons!" warnings on old maps, the purpose of this booklet is to advise researchers where trouble may lurk. The chapters do not pretend to cover all aspects of such hazards, but each chapter will include a brief list of "Useful Published Sources" where more complete information may be found. If your search brings you into a high-risk area these are the books that can help you learn about the types of mistakes you may make and, hopefully, show you how to avoid them. These books should also lead you to other books on the same subject, some in their bibliographies, others sitting beside them on library shelves.

To start you off, an excellent all purpose guide-book to that foreign country, *the past*, is by Daniel Pool: *What Jane Austen Ate and Charles Dickens Knew: from fox hunting to whist—the facts of daily life in nineteenth-century England*, (New York, London, Toronto, etc.: Simon & Schuster, c1993).

Althea Douglas
Ottawa, 1996

Chapter 2

IT DEPENDS ON WHAT YOU MEAN BY CANADA

Canada West is not in Western Canada

> Great-great-grandfather said he was born in Canada, about 1840. How do I get a birth certificate?

This query is a hazard in two ways. Official Birth Certificates are not available as early as 1840. The real trap, however, is the fact that what today is called **CANADA** was not a country until 1867.

In 1840, where and what was Canada? In 1860, when great-grandfather told a census taker his age and place of birth, what did *he* mean by Canada? If he offered this same information in 1880, could it mean something different? These are questions genealogists must ask—and find the answers to.

The northern portion of North America that on today's maps is labelled **CANADA** has been called by many different names over the last four centuries and the dates when the names change can be important to researchers. Let's run through those centuries, starting with the explorers and colonists from France who sailed up the Saint Lawrence River into the Great Lakes, and then down the Mississippi.

Canada, a part of New France

NEW FRANCE usually means all the French possessions in continental North America: the crescent from Cape Breton to the mouth of the Mississippi. French colonists distinguished between Acadia, Canada and Louisiana.

> **ACADIA**, or *Acadie* (now the Maritime Provinces) thrusts out into the Atlantic towards Newfoundland where both English and French fishermen had settlements.

> **CANADA** was the colony along the St Lawrence from above Montreal to some hundred miles below Quebec City. Here lived the *canadiens* and *canadiennes*. New England lay to the south along the Atlantic.

3

LOUISIANA, on mid-eighteenth century maps, is sometimes the whole area drained by the Mississippi River system and explored by the French, at that time largely unsettled. On later maps it becomes smaller and smaller. Rupert's Land lay to the north and west.

RUPERT'S LAND, what is that? When the Company of Adventurers of England trading into Hudson's Bay received their Royal charter in 1670, Charles II granted his cousin, Prince Rupert, and his fellow adventurers a monopoly over all the lands draining into the Hudson Bay (NOTE: the Company is Hudson's Bay, the body of water, Hudson Bay). At the time, no one knew that Rupert's Land covered over a million and a half square miles, stretching from Labrador to the Rockies and, in the west, extending well below the 49th parallel. It formed the northern and western limits to New France. We will return to Rupert's land when we move west.

Acadia *vs* Nova Scotia

NOVA SCOTIA (the mainland, not Cape Breton) was disputed territory in the 17th century; settled by the French but claimed by the British, who gained title to the peninsula in 1713 with the *Treaty of Utrecht*, but who would not control all of Acadia until the *Treaty of Paris*, in 1763.

ACADIA, collectively the French settlements in the peninsula we now know as Nova Scotia and southern New Brunswick, included two islands:

ÎLE-ROYALE, which, after 1763, became **CAPE BRETON** and a part of Nova Scotia. Cape Breton had a separate government between 1784 and 1820, after which it again became a part of Nova Scotia.

ÎLE-ST-JEAN was the other French Island which, after 1763, was called the Island of St John and, in 1798, renamed **PRINCE EDWARD ISLAND**.

During the 18th century, the British gradually took control of Acadia, expelled many of the French, and brought in settlers that hopefully would be loyal to the British Crown.
(See **A FRAMEWORK OF USEFUL DATES** listed on both inside covers).

NEW BRUNSWICK was separated from Nova Scotia on 19 November 1784, and its boundaries have not changed except for the disputed line along the border with Maine, finally established in 1842 by the *Ashburton Treaty*.

Canada becomes Quebec

After the British subdued the French colony of Canada, it was renamed the **PROVINCE OF QUEBEC** (7 October 1764). By then, the colony included portions of what is now southern Ontario into which refugee Loyalists flocked after the American War of Independence ended in 1783.

Canada — Upper and Lower

On 26 December 1791, the British, perhaps as a Christmas present to newly-arrived English-speaking colonists, split the colony in two: **LOWER CANADA** and **UPPER CANADA**. Each had their own legislature and their own (quite different) civil law codes and rules of land tenure. English-speaking residents were a minority in Lower Canada, but only just, and they objected to "French" domination of the Legislature. If the provinces were united, they would be a majority.

The Canadas — East and West

From 10 February 1841 to 30 June 1867, under the Act of Union, Upper and Lower Canada were joined in a short-lived, uneasy union with a single government, as the **PROVINCE OF CANADA**. Parliament met at different times in Kingston, Montreal, Quebec City and Toronto. The two regions were referred to as **CANADA EAST** and **CANADA WEST**, or sometimes simply as **THE CANADAS**.

The Dominion of Canada and How it Grew

Confederation, in 1867, saw the Canadas again become separate provinces, **QUEBEC** and **ONTARIO**. That year the Province of Canada, Nova Scotia and New Brunswick agreed (under British pressure) to join together. At Westminster, the British Parliament passed the British North America Act and the **DOMINION OF CANADA** came into being on 1 July 1867.

Those dates are important to researchers. References to Upper and Lower Canada imply a time before 1841, Canada West and Canada East existed between 1841 and Confederation and any reference to Ontario implies a time after 1867. A word of warning: well into this century people in the Maritimes might refer disparagingly, or resentfully, to "Upper Canadians", by which they meant anyone from the Canadas, and especially the triangle of wealth and power between Montreal, Ottawa and Toronto.

> ▶ When someone born before 1867 tells an American Census taker they were "born in Canada" they usually meant Ontario, but *might* mean Quebec. Few people born in New Brunswick or Prince Edward Island, and no Nova Scotian, would say that until this century.

QUEBEC means Quebec, perhaps the post-conquest colony with borders that extend across the Ottawa River, perhaps Lower Canada, or Canada East; but make sure the reference is not to Quebec City itself. There are names for regions of Quebec that you may not see on a map: the Eastern Townships or, simply, The Townships (now termed *l'Estrie*) along the border with the USA; the Laurentians (hills north of Montreal); the North Shore (east of Quebec City along the St. Lawrence); l'Outaouais (east side of the Ottawa river and its Quebec tributaries); and the Gaspé peninsula.

Do not make the mistake of assuming that the inhabitants of Quebec were all French-speaking. Quebec City and Montreal were the ports of entry for most immigrants from the British Isles, and settlers from the United States moved north along every water route in search of land. At the time of Confederation, Montreal was more than half English-speaking, Quebec City about 45 percent, the Eastern Townships were overwhelmingly "English", and people of English, Scotch and Irish origin settled in the Gaspé and along both sides of the Ottawa River.

Nor should you assume Ontario was exclusively "English". The French had settled there long before the British arrived; they remained, multiplied and spread to the west with the fur trade. In Glengarry, most highland settlers had the Gaelic, and many German-speaking Loyalists and disbanded mercenaries took up land in Upper Canada. Nova Scotia had a similar mix.

By the Sea — the Atlantic

MARITIME PROVINCES is a collective term, normally meaning Nova Scotia, New Brunswick and Prince Edward Island.

NEWFOUNDLAND AND LABRADOR, the oldest British colony in North America, joined Canada in 1949, after which you will find journalists and political scientists talking about "Atlantic Canada".

ATLANTIC CANADA means all four "Atlantic Provinces": Newfoundland and Labrador, New Brunswick, Nova Scotia (to which Cape Breton Island **is** attached by a causeway) and **THE ISLAND** (Prince Edward Island). When someone refers to **THE ROCK** they mean Newfoundland. Many Newfoundlanders still consider themselves Newfoundlanders first and Canadians second.

Heading West

EASTERN CANADA and **WESTERN CANADA** are relative terms. So far we have been speaking about "The East" and/or "Central Canada", but perceptions depend on where you live. To a Nova Scotian, Winnipeg, the capital of Manitoba, represents "The West" of Canada; to a British Columbian it is almost "The East". In Winnipeg, people know it is over 1100 air miles to either Vancouver or Halifax. Some also know that the French built Fort Rouge there in 1738, before Halifax was founded in 1746 or Capt George Vancouver entered Burrard Inlet in 1792. The North West Company built Fort Gibraltar on "The Forks" in 1805; its rival the Hudson's Bay Company erected Fort Douglas in 1812; and, in that same year, the Earl of Selkirk's first settlers arrived at the junction of the Red and Assiniboine Rivers.

Here be Dragons!

Remember Rupert's Land?

When the Dominion of Canada came into being in 1867, the Hudson's Bay Company still owned over one third of the territory that is now Canada. The Red River Colony was a tiny settlement in the vast area still called Rupert's Land. However, in 1869-70, Great Britain encouraged the Company to sell much of Rupert's Land to the new Dominion and, on 11 May 1870, the Company was paid £300,000. It kept only a few million acres of land around Company Posts and in the fertile belt.

That same year, the area around the Red River Settlement was erected into the **PROVINCE OF MANITOBA** (an area much smaller than it is today). The remaining lands, called the **NORTHWEST TERRITORIES**, were divided into various administrative "Districts" named Mackenzie, Athabaska, Alberta, Saskatchewan, Assiniboia, Keewatin and Ungava. In 1905, the Districts of Saskatchewan, Assiniboia, Alberta, Athabaska and part of Mackenzie (south of the 60th parallel) were amalgamated to form two Provinces, **ALBERTA** and **SASKATCHEWAN**. Finally, in 1912, the eastern part of Keewatin was assigned to Ontario, and Ungava (that part of Rupert's Land to the east of Hudson and James Bay) went to Quebec.

The **YUKON** Territory was established in 1897 because of the Gold Rush, and the borders of what remains of the Northwest Territories are still being shifted and changed. **NUNAVUT** will become a separate Territory in 1999.

By the Sea — the Pacific

Out on Vancouver's Island an outpost of the fur trade developed and was assigned to the Hudson's Bay Company on condition they colonize it. When gold was discovered on the mainland in 1858, that area saw an influx of settlers and police. There were boundary disputes between Britain and the United States but, by 1863, mainland areas—formerly called New Caledonia and Columbia—were amalgamated into **BRITISH COLUMBIA** with its present mainland boundaries.

The Colony of **VANCOUVER ISLAND** was annexed to British Columbia on 19 November 1866. British Columbia entered Confederation in 1871, on the condition that a railway be built to join it to the rest of the country.

Today you must deal with ten provinces and two territories going on three, as well as a Federal Government. For genealogists, the problem is to determine in which region the records of ancestors may be found, and this changes over time. Bear in mind that each of these British North American colonies that came together under the Canadian umbrella have their own history. Many had their own elected legislatures, which they kept. Each holds different records in their archives and other repositories, and each maintains their own vital records. After 1867 there was, in addition, an overall Canadian Federal Government, with a capital city, Ottawa. Here the National Archives of Canada not only keep the records of the Dominion of Canada, but some from the earlier Canadas, as well as an assembly of copied or filmed records that relate to Canada from other parts of the world. Their holdings are detailed in numerous publications, the most useful for genealogists being the free booklet *Tracing Your Ancestors in Canada*, last revised in 1991. It can be obtained by writing to The National Archives of Canada, 395 Wellington St., Ottawa, ON K1A 0N3. The booklet contains the addresses of all the provincial and territorial archives and offices of civil registration.

USEFUL PUBLISHED SOURCES

The Oxford Companion to Canadian History and Literature, Norah Story, ed.
Toronto, London, New York: Oxford University Press, 1968, c1967.
>Here you will find detailed accounts of most Canadian political divisions and places referred to in this brief survey.

The Fitzhenry & Whiteside Book of Canadian Facts & Dates,
compiler: Jay Myers; revised & updated by L. Hoffman and F. Sutherland.
Richmond Hill, ON: Fitzhenry & Whiteside, c1986; revised edition, c1991.

Historical Atlas of Canada, three editions.
editor: Donald G.G. Kerr; cartographer: Maj. C.C.J. Bond.
Don Mills, ON: Thomas Nelson & Sons (Canada) Ltd., c1960, c1966, 1975.
>A slim single volume, probably more widely available than the newer 3-volume publication of the same name. Excellent for finding the dates and changes made in territorial boundaries of Canada.

Here be Dragons!

Historical Atlas of Canada. Volume I: From the Beginning to 1800 ; Volume II: The Land Transformed 1800-1891 ; Volume III: Addressing the Twentieth Century 1891-1961, cartographer & designer: Geoffrey J. Matthews; with separate editors for each volume. Vol.1: R. Cole Harris; Vol.2: R. Louis Gentilcore, et al; Vol.3: Donald Kerr, Deryck Holdsworth. Toronto, Buffalo, London: University of Toronto Press, 1987, 1993 and 1990.

> Vol.I, Plate 51: maps the Seigneuries in the French Colony of Canada; Vol.II, Plate 5: illustrates the territorial divisions of Canada in 1891; Vol.II, Plate 21: shows the development of British Columbia, and Vol.III, Plate 2: illustrates how Rupert's Land was divided among Canadian Provinces. These volumes are invaluable sources for tracing exploration, migration and settlement patterns,

> Subsequent references will cite specific Plates in the *Historical Atlas,* using this short title and the Volume number.

The Encyclopedia of Canada, general editor: W. Stewart Wallace. 6 vols. Toronto: University Associates of Canada Ltd, 1935-37; registered edition, 1940; 2nd edition, 1948.

> Edited by a noted historian and librarian just before World War II, the entries are now a valuable "Guide to the Recent Past". Town entries list the railroads that served each community, and help to differentiate between places (and people) of the same name. As well, there are brief histories of the fur trade "Forts", the religious orders that served in early Canada, and how various Canadian religious denominations evolved. Subsequent references will be to *Encyclopedia of Canada* plus the topic of the entry.

Canada and its Provinces: a history of the Canadian people and their institutions ..., general editors: Adam Shortt & Arthur G. Doughty. 23 vols. Toronto and Edinburgh: Publishers Association of Canada Ltd, 1913-1917.

> Very detailed history of Canada, its provinces and people, divided into geographic areas. Volume 23 is a general index providing, as well, the source documents used and a bibliography, along with a chronological outline, historical tables and lists of names. Adam Shortt was the chairman of the Board of Historical Publications at the, then, Public Archives of Canada and Arthur Doughty was the Dominion Archivist.

Chapter 3

THE TOWNSHIP TRAP

Is Hamilton East or West of Toronto?

Consider the following:

> Amos A----- is listed among the settlers in Hamilton, on Lot 29, Concession 2. But when you check a map showing the land divisions where Hamilton city is now, Concession 2 ends well before lot 29.

> In 1832, Mary B-----, daughter of George B----- of York, was married to John D----- of Toronto. Was the bride from the town of York, York Township, or York County? In any case, York did not become Toronto until 1834. Where was the groom's residence?

> George C----- 's two sons took up land in Mariposa. Humorist Stephen Leacock modeled his fictional town of Mariposa on Orillia, but was there also a real village?

The answer to these puzzles is the simple term — **TOWNSHIP**. When Ontario was first settled there were few villages or towns. When asked where they lived, settlers usually gave the name of their Township. Amos A----- settled in Hamilton Township, east of the city of Toronto, and not in Hamilton, the city west of Toronto. Toronto was also a Township in Peel County, well before the name was given to "muddy York", and Mariposa is a Township in Victoria County in southern Ontario.

The Township is the basic survey and administrative division of land in Ontario. After the American Revolution, as refugee Loyalists fled north, British-trained surveyors divided the unsettled land (Crown land) into orderly square **TOWNSHIPS**, sliced them into parallel **CONCESSIONS** (or **RANGES**) with a road allowance between each, and then divided each Concession into individual **LOTS** (usually 200 acres). Individual farms are identified by Township, Concession number and Lot number(s). Thus, while the borders of Administrative Districts or Counties have been, and still are, political variables, Township borders have remained fairly constant until quite recently.

Here be Dragons!

There are hundreds of townships in Ontario, named after almost every familiar British town, county, and nobleman, as well as a lot of less well-known local politicians. Worse still, they share these names with towns, villages and counties that are often in different parts of the province, or even in another province. Longueuil, a city on the St. Lawrence across from Montreal, shares its name with Longueuil Township in *Prescott County*, on the Ottawa River at the far-eastern tip of Ontario. The *Town of Prescott*, however, is in Augusta Township, Grenville County, and *Prescott Township* is in the Algoma District in northern Ontario,

Most maps from the 19th century show townships, but few modern road maps include the divisions; on many you are lucky to find counties marked. In Ontario, however, one exception is *The Ontario Transportation Map Series*, distributed by MapArt Corporation, 72 Bloor Street East, Oshawa, ON. L1H 3M2, and also available from OGS. This series of large-scale road maps covers much of southern Ontario, showing not only townships, but often concession and lot divisions.

Townships *vs* Seigneuries

Quebec also has **TOWNSHIPS**, as well as **SEIGNEURIES** and a few **FIEFS**, and, naturally, a number of these townships have the same names as Ontario townships (Chester, Dundee, Inverness, Leeds, Warwick, etc., as examples).

In New France, the land along the Saint Lawrence River and its tributaries was granted by the French King (through his Governors) to Seigneurs. These grants extended inland from the various waterways making an irregular pattern. Richard Colebrook Harris's *The Seigneurial System in Early Canada* explains the many complex details of this system of land tenure. Within the Seigneuries, (fiefs were usually smaller), the inhabitants belonged to a **PARISH**, usually named for a Saint, and vital records were kept by the Parish Priest. When parishes were named for a popular Saint, they usually added the name of the Seigneury or another identifying term: Ste-Anne-de Beaupré, Ste-Anne-de-Bellevue, Ste-Anne-des-Monts, Ste-Anne-des-Lacs, not to be confused with Ste-Anne-du-Lac (Labelle County) and Ste-Anne-du-Lac (Megantic County).

After the British conquest, when English-speaking settlers began arriving in Quebec, the hilly land along the US border was surveyed into block-shaped townships. Three rows march parallel with the border but, closer to the rivers, the surveyors had to adjust the townships to fit around the irregular Seigneurial lands. The grid pattern is less dominant than in Ontario, although the townships usually have parallel **RANGES** divided into Lots. In the townships, land tenure was freehold in the English manner and, because of this, English-speaking settlers usually moved through the French seigneuries into "The Townships" — more generally called the **EASTERN TOWNSHIPS**. These also attracted American settlers from across the border to the south.

SEIGNEURIES and **TOWNSHIPS** were grouped together into Judicial Districts and Counties, but the borders have changed many times. I summarized the changes in the Eastern Townships' boundaries (in English) in *Canadian Genealogist*, vol.10, no.2 (June 1988), using maps based in part on the endpaper map from C.P. de Volpi and P.H. Scowan's, *The Eastern Townships: A Pictorial Record*, (Montreal, 1962).

Townships in The Maritimes

In Nova Scotia, the New Englanders who came in the 1760s and 1770s also called their scattered settlements Townships, and regulated community affairs through Town Meetings. After the American War of Independence, the British quickly put an end to such potential hotbeds of revolution and, in both Nova Scotia and New Brunswick, the County is now the basic administrative unit. In New Brunswick, counties are divided into **CIVIL PARISHES** and these township-sized divisions show up most commonly as census districts. Note that both these provinces have a Kings County, Queens County, and Victoria County, while Prince Edward Island has Kings, Queens, and Prince Counties.

When Prince Edward Island was surveyed, these three counties were subdivided into *numbered* townships (67 in all) of about 20,000 acres each. In London, in 1767, these townships were distributed by a lottery to people "deserving Royal patronage" and so are now termed "Lots". The numbering of the **LOTS** is somewhat haphazard, but there is a map in the *Genealogist's Handbook for Atlantic Canada Research*, edited by Terrence M. Punch, CG(C), as well as an explanation of the complex land records.

Here be Dragons!

Newfoundland and Labrador have no Township hazards. There the Crown Land grants are divided by **BAYS** or **COASTS**. The harbours, islands, coves and outports, some with distinctive names, are the points of reference.

Rupert's Land

After Confederation, it was apparent that if Canada was to hold on to the Hudson's Bay Company's lands, they would have to be surveyed and settled. In western Canada, this system is blessedly simple. The new country acted quickly, meridian lines were established and the western lands were surveyed into **RANGES**, **TOWNSHIPS**, and **SECTIONS**, all numbered. The regular grid can be seen in the *Historical Atlas of Canada, Vol.III*, Plate 17: (Peopling the Prairies). The usual land holding was a quarter-section.

USEFUL PUBLISHED SOURCES

Genealogist's Handbook for Atlantic Canada Research,
editor: Terrence M Punch, CG(C).
Boston: New England Historic Genealogical Society, 1989.
> Includes a section on each Atlantic province, compiled by a noted local genealogist, with maps and explanations of land divisions.

The Seigneurial System in Early Canada: a geographic study,
by Richard Colebrook Harris.
Madison, Milwaukee and London: The University of Wisconsin Press, 1966;
Québec: Les Presses de l'Université Laval, 1968, c1966.
Montreal/Kingston: McGill-Queen's University Press, 1984 reprint.

Canada Before Confederation: a study in historical geography,
by R. Cole Harris and John Warkentin; cartographer: Miklos Printher.
New York, London, Toronto: Oxford University Press, 1974.
Ottawa: Carleton University Press, 1991 reprint.
> A valuable survey of how and why the country was settled: including varieties of land divisions; how our ancestors changed the face of the land; what they built; what they grew, where and when; and how settlement moved across the continent before Confederation.

The British Dominions in North America; or a topographical and statistical description of the Provinces of Lower and Upper Canada, New Brunswick, Nova Scotia, the Islands of Newfoundland, Prince Edward and Cape Breton; ..., by Joseph Bouchette. 3 vols in 2,

London: Longman, Rees, Orme, Brown, Green & Longman, 1832.
New York: AMS Press, 1968 reprint.
Ottawa: Canadian Institute for Historical Microreproductions, microfiche, 1984
>   Available in the Rare Book Section of many reference libraries. Vol. I has particularly useful tabulations of the Townships surveyed and granted in Lower Canada after 1795. The CIHM microfiche are also available at a number of research libraries: Fiche # 48010/11/12.

A Topographical Description of the Province of Lower Canada, with remarks upon Upper Canada, and on the relative connexion of both provinces with the United States of America, by Joseph Bouchette.
London: printed for the author and published by W. Faden, 1815
St Lambert, QC: Canada East Reprints, facsimile edition, 1973.

Townships of the Province of Ontario Canada: a complete index of the townships in all the counties & districts of Ontario (includes 10 Area Maps), compilers: M.E. Gartner and C.F. Prong.
North Bay, ON: Nipissing District Branch, OGS, 1992.
>   This essential research tool also explains recent changes resulting from Ontario's development of Municipal Regions.

Index to Township Plans of the Canadian West,
compilers: Guy Poulin and Francine Cadieux.
Ottawa: National Map Collection, Public Archives of Canada, 1974.
>   Explains in detail the surveying process across the west of Canada.

Post Offices of Alberta, 1876-1986, by Neil Hughes.
Edmonton, AB: privately printed, 1986.
>   While essentially a book for philatelists who collect post-office cancellations, the "Introduction" includes a simple and clear explanation of western land divisions.

Here be Dragons!

An Upper Canadian Address Consisted of Township, Concession, Lot Number
In the early days, surveying started where settlement started, that is, at the edge of a body of water. Surveyors commonly laid out the Concessions parallel to it. The lots along the water were termed "broken front" and, where the water's edge was very irregular and the Concession had less than the standard number of lots, the first couple of Concessions might be labeled "A" and "B". Townships further inland might have Concession lines perpendicular to those in regions surveyed earlier.

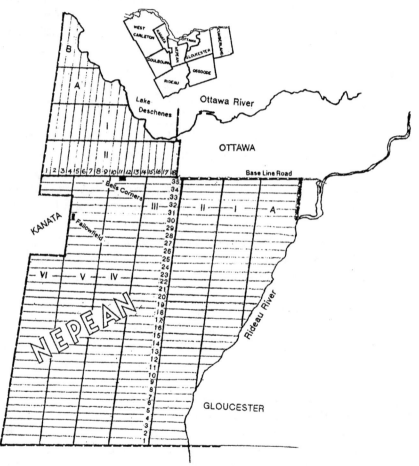

The Township of Nepean in Carleton County is bounded, in part, by the Ottawa River and the Rideau River. Early surveyors started to lay out Concessions along both the "Ottawa Front" and the "Rideau Front". While the City of Ottawa has absorbed part of the original Township, these two systems still meet at Base Line Road.

Chapter 4

THE SAME NAME and the CHANGED NAME HAZARDS

A rose by any other name ...

> "Uniqueness may even make a name otherwise not good
> seem pleasing, as *Medicine Hat, Burnt Church*. No matter
> how excellent a name may be in itself, it is cheapened by
> extension to other places." [1]

Family historians will endorse Dr. Ganong's sentiments, for the same-name
hazard exists all across the continent. His essay also discusses that other
problem: how names may "*persist or become extinct*", and why there may be
"deliberate replacement as a place grows in importance and culture" (p.8).

When Newark, the first capital of Upper Canada, was renamed Niagara-on-
the-Lake, only the dozen or so Newarks in the United States remained to
confuse researchers. In 1829, Quebec's York County was subdivided into
Vaudreuil, Deux-Montagnes and Ottawa counties. When the Town of York
was incorporated as the city of Toronto in 1834, this removed another "York"
from the long list, but the name was quickly appropriated by tiny Nelles
Settlement in Haldimand County. That county, bordering on Lake Erie, was
named for Sir Frederick Haldimand, as was Haldimand Township in North-
umberland County bordering on Lake Ontario. It should hardly come as a
surprise to find another Haldimand out on the tip of the Gaspé peninsula.

The Same or Similar Names

So when great-aunt Mary assures you that her grandfather was born in
Haldimand and her father in Waterloo, take care. There is a town of Waterloo
in Ontario (Upper Canada/Canada West), north of Toronto in Waterloo
Township, Waterloo County (now called the Regional Municipality of

---

[1]   W.F. Ganong, "An essay towards an understanding of the principles of place
name nomenclature", first published *Transactions of the Royal Society of
Canada*, II, 1896, pp.177-214, quoted from a revised version, *Geographical
names of New Brunswick*, comp. Alan Rayburn (Ottawa: Surveys & Mapping
Branch, Energy, Mines and Resources Canada, 1975), p.4.

Waterloo), but there is another Waterloo in Shefford Township, Shefford County, in the Eastern Townships of Quebec (Lower Canada/Canada East), once an English-speaking area south of Montreal. Three miles north-west of Kingston, Ontario, another Waterloo was renamed Cataraqui by the Post Office in 1868. You can also find Waterloo, Nova Scotia; a Waterloo Corner and "Waterloo Settlement" in New Brunswick; and towns called Waterloo in Arkansas, California, Illinois, Iowa, Michigan, New Hampshire, New York, and Pennsylvania, among other states in the U.S.

Queen Victoria gave her name to the capital of British Columbia, but it is also found in Victoria Beach in Manitoba; Victoriaville, Arthabaska Co., in Quebec; Victoria Beach and Victoria Bridge in Nova Scotia; and Victoria in Prince Edward Island. When you check F.E. Carter's *Place Names of Ontario* [2] ,the author numbers nine geographic locations called Victoria, with close to three pages of "Victoria This" and "Victoria That" names. "Cheapened" indeed! Dr. Ganong would not approve.

Same Sounding Name

When grandmother said "Saint John" did she mean Saint John, New Brunswick, St John's, Newfoundland, or St Johns (Saint-Jean), Quebec? They can sound very similar when grandmother is reminiscing. St John could even be the township in the Cochrane District of Ontario, or it could refer to the river. Did grandmother's family live "along", or "up" or "beside" the river Saint John? Such meaningful words can drop out of memory over a century.

Living on a River

When a region was opened up by lumbering, the waterways were used to move the cut logs, and people lived along the banks of these rivers. In New Brunswick, references to "Mirimichi" are not to a town but to the watershed region draining into the river and, so, to settlements and farms all along the banks of the river and some of its tributaries. After the devastating Mirimichi fire in 1825, some inhabitants moved to Ontario, taking the name Mirimichi

---

[2]   London, ON: Phelps Publishing Co., 1984, 2 vols.

with them. Later, the location was renamed Pembroke [3] and remains so today. Here, in the Ottawa Valley, other rivers also gave names to settled areas. The *Bonnechère* (pronounced "Boncher") River on the Ontario side of the Ottawa River and *Rivière Noire* (Black River) on the Quebec side became official census districts. By 1871, *Rivière Noire* had six divisions.

For the 1881 and 1891 census returns, one must look under "Unorganized Territory" [4]. Such "unorganized", lumber-based communities shifted as the land was cleared and proved unfarmable, or if there was a forest fire. Religious comfort might be brought by missionaries, sent upriver in the summer by canoe, or in winter by sled, but not in spring during the log drives. Look for marriages and baptisms in the records of churches in the settled parishes downstream, or in the records of county Justices of the Peace, for they too performed marriages.

Translated names

To return for a moment to Black River or *Rivière Noire* in Pontiac County, Quebec: be aware that in the nineteenth century, when English-speaking people were in the majority in several parts of Quebec, place names like Black River, or St Johns, or even Three Rivers, were commonly given in English. In this century, as the English left and the French moved in, many places named for early "English" settlers, were given "Holy Names" like Saint-Paul-d'Abbotsford, Saint-Joachim-de-Shefford, Saint-Étienne-de-Bolton and Saint-Ignace-de-Stanbridge. Finally with the current Language Laws now strictly enforced, any part of any English place name that can be translated has been changed to French. This should not present difficulties for the words are very similar: *lac* = lake; *rivière* = river; *mont* = mountain (or hill); *cap* = cape; *îsle* = island; *chute* = falls; *rapide* = rapids; *ville* = town or city (but not *un village*); etc. The Eastern Townships have become *Les Cantons de l'Est* or *l'Estrie*.

---

[3] *Geographical names of New Brunswick*, p.184.

[4] *Catalogue of Census Returns on Microfilm 1666-1891*,
Thomas A. Hillman, compiler, Ottawa: Supply and Services Canada, 1987

Changed Names

The town of York resumed its original name, Toronto, when it was incorporated as a city in 1834; Bytown became Ottawa in 1857. Berlin was renamed Kitchener during World War I, and there are many more such name changes across the country. Brenda Dougall Merriman lists over two dozen Ontario changes in *Genealogy in Ontario* and gives sources for finding further information. She also explains the artificial "counties" created as enumeration districts for the 1871 and later censuses, identifies the early numbered townships, and her book includes a series of valuable maps giving the names of the various administrative Districts of Upper Canada, then of Canada West, and then of Ontario prior to 1968 with the formation of a number of Regional Government districts.

Men of Upper Canada: Militia Nominal Rolls, 1828-1829, includes a set of maps showing the names and boundaries of Miltia Districts (which sometimes differ from political divisions) and a table giving the Township name and its County in 1828-1829, and the County name in the 20th century, some of which changed.

Geographical names of New Brunswick reprints Dr. Ganong's two brilliant essays on place names, which are well worth reading regardless of where your family interests lie, and, as well, offers a complete version of "Sweet Maiden of Quoddy", a delightful introduction to place names of Native origin. There are cross-references for obsolete names, eg. "*Parr Town*: See Saint John" or "*Kingsville* see Milford"; "*Pleasant Point* see Milford"; "*St. Marysville* see Milford"; not to be confused, of course, with the Milford in Ontario!

Gazetteers for other provinces offer similar help, if not the poetry. Do use them; it will save a lot of fruitless searching. First, consider *all* the places mentioned in family stories in the complete context of the tale. If a place name cannot be found on a modern map, note what other names are associated with it. Read Chapter 12, "Some Thoughts on Geography", ponder how people moved about in the past, then search Gazetteers and *Place names of ------- to determine which province, county, and town or township is meant.

USEFUL PUBLISHED SOURCES

Gazetteer of Canada. [Name of Province],
> At least one volume for each Province or Territory. These are available in most libraries, and are regularly updated by a government Permanent Committee on Geographic Names (which, itself, has borne various names over the years) through the Department of Energy, Mines and Resources (now Natural Resources Canada). This Committee maintains records of all Canadian geographical names and name changes.

Post Offices of ... [Name of Province],
> Labours of love, these volumes were published for collectors of postal cancellations (many examples are included), and to preserve the memory of now-closed or "ghost" offices. F.E. Carter notes that in Ontario, of over 8,000 post offices, only 1300 were active in 1986. We are also reminded that the first Postmaster got to name the office and often named it after themself, so check your family's place names. The first three books include the names of postmasters, as well as opening and terminating dates and some history of the office. The information in the others varies.

Ghost and Post Offices of Ontario, by Floreen Ellen Carter.
Oakville, ON: Personal Impressions Publishing, 1986.

Post Offices of New Brunswick, 1783-1930, by George E. MacManus.
Toronto: Jim A. Hennock Ltd., 1986, c1984.

The Post Offices of British Columbia, by George H. Melvin.
Vernon, BC: privately printed, 1972.

Canada Post Offices, 1755-1895: for all provinces except Newfoundland,
by Frank W. Campbell.
Boston: Quarterman Publications Inc., 1972, c1963.

Les Bureaux de Poste du Québec, by Anatole Walker.
Montreal: Le Marché philatélique de Montréal, 1987.

Northwest Territories Postal Cancellations, 1907-1986,
by Kevin O'Reilly.   Toronto: The Unitrade Press, 1987.

Post Offices of Alberta, 1876-1986, by Neil Hughes.
Edmonton, AB: privately printed, 1986.

Noms et Lieux du Québec: dictionnaire illustré,
compiled by Commission de toponymie.
Québec: Les publications du Québec, 1994.
> A beautiful volume with maps giving the most current administrative divisions.

Geographical Names of New Brunswick, Toponymy Study 2.
compiler: Alan Rayburn.
Ottawa: Surveys & Mapping Branch, Energy Mines & Resources Canada, 1975.

Genealogy In Ontario: searching the records, 3rd edition, revised & enlarged,
by Brenda Dougall Merriman.
Toronto: Ontario Genealogical Society, 1996.
> Includes a set of maps showing the early administrative districts and various county divisions in Ontario (pp. viii-xiv) and lists of ambiguous and changed names in her Introduction to the volume.

Men of Upper Canada: militia nominal rolls, 1828-1829,
editors: Bruce S. Elliott, Dan Walker, Fawne Stratford-Devai;
with maps by Peter D.B. Mérey.
Toronto: Ontario Genealogical Society, 1995.

Inventory of Cemeteries in Ontario: a genealogical research guide,
compiler: Vera Ronnow. Toronto: Ontario Genealogical Society, 1987.
> Includes a short listing of "Place Names in Ontario", pp. 190-248.
> This work is currently being revised and expected to be republished in 1997, complete with a second volume of township maps on which the location of each cemetery is identified.

For other books of place names in individual provinces, check your library catalogue under *Gazetteer of -----*, *Place Names of -----* or *Geographical Names of -----*.

Chapter 5

SOME NOTES ON 18th- and 19th-CENTURY DOCUMENTS

Never trust a transcript

Clearly, Medieval and Elizabethan writing is difficult for the average person to read unless they take a course in palaeography. On the other hand, when researchers encounter documents from the 18th and early 19th century, the writing looks so much like our own that the tendency is to plunge right in —perhaps into an orthographic trap.

By the mid-18th century, people wrote much the way we do now, but there are some differences that can cause errors. Moreover, old fashioned writing habits seem to have persisted in North America long after they disappeared in Britain. Perhaps this was because there were fewer teachers, and one or two who stuck to the old ways could influence a second and even a third generation.

For example, be aware that there is a confusing form of written "**e**" that looks like an "**o**". The name really was Henry, not *Honry*, as one family member insisted when she looked at the register entry. Everyone knows about the long "**s**" that looks like an "**f**" when it appears in print. When it turns up in handwritten text, however, it is not always recognized. In particular, it persisted when writing a double "**ss**" long after it was dropped from type fonts.

Ca*f*s, Cap, Cals or Cass?

In some early 19th-century letters I once edited, a mother fed her delicate baby what we first read as *apes' milk*. This caused some raised eyebrows until we recognized what she had written was "asses' milk", using the long "*f*" and a normal "s" that together look quite like a "**p**". A*f*ses' milk became a joke, but misreading a family name is not so funny.

Recently, looking for a family named *Cass* in various published indexes to parish registers in eastern Ontario and western Quebec, I found that Cass had not only been read and indexed as *Carr*, but since several priests used the old-fashioned, long-short double **ss**, Ca*f*s also turned up as *Cap* and once as

Cals. Remember, an index is just that. It is subject to human error. Check the original manuscript whenever possible.

18th- and 19th-century spelling—even after Dr Johnson published his Dictionary—was, for the most part, phonetic and so highly variable. In pioneer settlements, few people were fully literate, even if they could sign their name to a document some clerk or lawyer drew up. Clerks and clergymen, census takers and compilers of directories wrote down what they heard—what people told them. They transcribed broad Scots, Irish brogue, French, German or Gaelic accents into official documents in English or French, and the informant was rarely capable of checking what they wrote.
(See Chapter 6: "Notes on Names".)

Paper was not the available commodity it is today. Official documents normally use a full sheet, but the promissory note your great-grandfather gave the local storekeeper may be on a small strip torn off a larger page—and the writing may be tiny and cramped. Except for squeezed-up words, however, most handwriting should not be difficult to decipher, though faded ink can be a problem, particularly when reading microfilmed records.

There are two tricks to dealing with mysterious words. Try pronouncing the letters phonetically, several times. Inspiration may strike. Or, if you are using microfilm, put a piece of paper on the screen and try tracing over the word. The hand may know better than the eye what the letters are. **NEVER** do this with an original manuscript unless you place a piece of glass or plexiglass over it first.

Two conventions accepted by scholars when transcribing handwritten manuscripts are the use of pointed brackets < > around doubtful readings of words, and square brackets [ ] to indicate the enclosed comments are your own, and not in the text being copied.

> e.g.: She told me her name was Al<ltoa>. [known to be: Althea]

Use these symbols when making notes; you will probably bless yourself two years later.

Postage before 1840

The world's first postage stamps were issued by Great Britain in May 1840. Before that date, the British postal service was surprisingly good, but the postage was paid by the recipient and calculated per sheet. The size of the sheet did not matter, so instead of envelopes, most letters were written on folded sheets and these were folded again and sealed, leaving a blank space on the back page for the address and postmarks.

To cram as much news as possible on the single sheet, some 19th-century letters might be cross-written. There was skill to this, and it is often much easier to read than you might think at first glance. Relax, let your eyes follow the lines, and your brain will separate out the text you want. However, I do not touch-type, and I find it easier to read this sort of letter aloud, into a tape recorder, and transcribe from that.

Abbreviations can be traps

When a letter or two are raised at the end of a word, it usually signifies a contraction or abbreviation. **Y^e**, the old form of *the*, was going out of fashion by the middle of the 18th century but **w^{th}** and **w^{ch}** are quite common. "John" may appear as **J^n** or **J^{no}**, but be careful not to confuse these with **Jo^n** or **Jo^{na}** for Jonathan. Remember **X** means Christ as in *Xian* (Christian) and *Xopher* (Christopher) — or *Xmas*.

Beware of the lazy parish clerk who uses "ditto" abbreviated to **D^o**. I found someone interpreting this as December when it actually referred back to June a few lines above. As well, be suspicious of ditto marks used by census takers, particularly regarding origin or birth-place.

Census ages, as well as those in obituaries, and even on tombstones, are also suspect. Tombstones, in particular, become weather-worn so an 8 may look like a 3, 4 become a 1, or 9 a 7. Genealogists learn to treat the ages given in census returns as an **APPROXIMATION** only. People forget, or lie, or just don't know and make a guess. Moving to a new place may take ten years off a man or woman's age. Some early census returns asked for the "age at next birthday", and this can lead you into error when calculating birth dates.

Entries in the family Bible of course are another matter, or are they? First, check the date of publication. The Bible may have been published some years **after** the dates of the first entries. Such entries may have been copied (or miscopied) into the new Bible from some other source. Be suspicious if entries are all in the same ink. The hand may be the same but different inks indicate different times of writing, and so probably contemporary with the event recorded. There is a Bible in my family, published some years after the dates of the first entries, which records one date that does not agree with the Parish register. Counting to nine explains why it was changed.

Finally:

> Most Respected Reader,
>   I humbly beseech you not to be annoyed or offended by the formal, not to say obsequious, language that was the standard polite form for letters, petitions and legal documents up until this century.
>   In the past, as in the future,
>   Please be assured, Honoured Sir or Madame,
>   I remain Your Most Humble
>   and obd^t Servt.

USEFUL PUBLISHED SOURCES

Examples of English Handwriting 1150-1750: with transcripts and translations, by Hilda E.P. Grieve.
Essex Record Office publication No. 21, 5th printing.
Chelmsford, ENG: Essex Educational Committee, Essex Record Office, 1981, (c1954).

How to read the handwriting and records of early America,
by E. Kay Kirkham.
Salt Lake City, UT: Deseret Book Co., 1964.
> Second edition of the handbook includes symbols, abbreviations, legal terminology, etc.

Handbook for Reading & Interpreting Old Documents; with examples from The Hudson's Bay Company Archives, by Elizabeth Briggs.
Winnipeg, MB: Manitoba Genealogical Society, 1992.

Particularly useful if you are working with numerical accounts. As well, there is a brief guide to unfamiliar terms and conventions from the past.

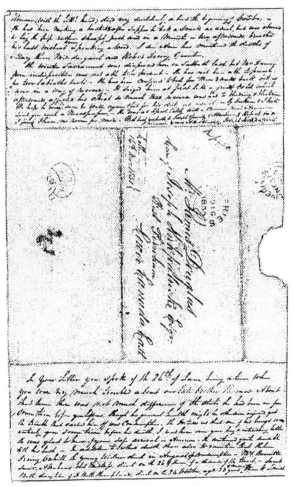

This four-page letter was written on a double folio sheet, folded in on itself, addressed and sealed. Removing the seal tore the edge of the second leaf.

A handwritten lease dated 30 March 1867

Chapter 6

SOME NOTES ON NAMES

Oral Traditions and Aural Spelling

Do not expect to find ancestors' names spelt exactly as you spell them today. The spelling of names is a variable everywhere and, in Canada, one must be constantly alert because of the intermingling of our two dominant language groups, French-speaking and English-speaking, as well as local pockets of Gaelic, German, Ukrainian, and others.

In the early isolated settlements, a majority of the population might well be illiterate. The original Loyalists and emigrants from England or Scotland could usually sign their name with a flourish, but their children, growing up in a back-woods settlement, with no schoolmaster, might well sign with **HIS/HER X MARK**. Until almost the end of the 19th century, in rural French Canada, the Priest, Seigneur and Notary were usually the only ones who could write.

If the writer's spelling was phonetic, and most was, some odd things turn up, and you may hear the echo of an ancestor's accent. Remember that settlers from the British Isles did not speak BBC standard English but, rather, brought across the Atlantic a variety of broad local dialects.

Imagine the potentials for misunderstanding—and misspellings—when, in 1776, an upper-class British officer, who wanted repairs made at Fort Lawrence in Nova Scotia, engaged a newly-arrived stonemason speaking broadest Yorkshire, a carpenter born and raised in New Hampshire, and perhaps a couple of French-speaking Acadians. Consider an English-speaking Irish priest taking down the family details required for the Parish register from a Gaelic-speaking Highland soldier, about to be disbanded at Quebec City, and the young Canadienne he wished to marry.

Beecham's pills and Eno's fruit-salts

When an ancestor migrates to a region where another language is spoken look for changes. Sometimes spelling is changed to ensure a name is given the familiar pronunciation. In French-speaking regions, for example, spelling "*Douglas*" with a double "**s**" — *Douglass* — means a Francophone will give the name a recognizable pronunciation instead of asking for a *Madame Dooglah*. Some Irish ancestors, originally named *Bridget*, started to spell it *Bridgette* when they came to Quebec so the Francophones would pronounce the "**et**". In English-speaking areas, on the other hand, French names are often anglicized. *Hénault*, or *Eneau*, can become *Eno*, *Thibault* changes to *Thebo* — same pronunciation, simpler spelling.

However, strange things happen to the spelling and pronunciation of French-Canadian family names down in New England. If you have never studied French (or your family's native language) and do not know how the original family name was pronounced back home, find someone who does and ask them. Until you know how a name like *Benoit* is pronounced, you may not recognize *Benwa* as an excellent phonetic variant spelling.

Saint's names are popular in French Quebec and the man known as *Xavier* or *Baptiste* will probably turn up in church records as "*François-Xavier*" or "*Jean-Baptiste*"; then when he moves to New England or Central Ontario, look for "*Frank*" or "*John*". If you were baptised *Ste-Rose-de-Lima*, wouldn't you call yourself *Rose*, or *Rosette*? And if you do not find your ancestors indexed under the name they used, say *Pierre* and *Sophie* (Peter and Sophy), look for a *Joseph-Pierre* and a *Marie-Sophie* (or M.-Sophie), for sometimes whole families are given Joseph or Marie as first names.

When searching for French ancestors in English records, always watch out for translations. *Joseph Leblanc* may become *Joe White*. A long search for a Madame Dubois ended when we found she was known as "*Mrs Wood*". A friend once told us his family translated their Italian name, *Campobello*, to *Beauchamp* when they came to Quebec. Move *Beauchamp* to England and it becomes the familiar *Beecham* of pill and symphony conductor fame.

During World War I, when Germany was **The Enemy**, some families found it expedient to make their name less German, translating *Battenberg* to *Mountbatten*, or *Schmidt* to *Smith*, for example.

The use of Alias, Dit, and Nicknames

In the early days in North America people had large families and infant mortality was low. A little simple arithmetic will show that if a couple has six sons, and the sons average four sons each, that makes 31 families all with the same surname, and many with the same personal name, you may be sure. Even if some sons and grandsons move away, something has to be done to identify which person is which.

An **ALIAS** or "*nickname*" that identifies an individual by some place association or physical attribute can become the name the community recognizes. In Scottish settlements this is often attached to the first or Christian name, so we find "*Black* " Donald McDonald; "*Red* " Donald McDonald; "*Silver*" Donald McDonald; Donald "*Demerara* " McDonald; and Donald "*the Mill*" McDonald. If you are really lucky, your immigrant Donald McDonald will be styled Donald McDonald (*Greenfield*), that being the place he came from in Scotland.

This last is more in keeping with the custom in French Canada where such identifying names are quite likely to become surnames. This may have grown out of the French custom of ignoring a family name for the more elegant **de** or **d'** before a title or name of an estate. In France, *de* implies land ownership and, so, aristocratic origins but, in actual fact, three small vineyards, owned by three brothers in Joigny, allowed Alexandre Piochard to call himself *Monsieur d'Arblay*, his older brother Louis Piochard to be the *Seigneur de Pommercourt*, and François Piochard to be known as *Monsieur de Blécy*. This also gave enough cachet that they could become officers in the French army.

In the lower ranks, French soldiers might have nicknames, or *noms de guerre*, that passed down to their descendants. Settlers could be identified by their French Province of origin, or some personal trait. The term usually found in Quebec is *dit* — meaning "called" (*dite* is the feminine) — as in "Eneau *dit* Portneuf". Occasionally *alias* is used. The family name may disappear if the sobriquet is widely accepted in the community; for example, our neighbours, the Jolicoeurs, actually descend from the family of Deveau *dit* Jolicoeur. These *dit* names can complicate searches, particularly if only one (*Jolicoeur*) is used and so-known in the community, while official records use the other (*Deveau*) first so that all entries are indexed by that name.

When searching in French sources, remember that **NOM** means surname (*nom de famille* = family name) while **PRÉNOM** is the personal (first or

Christian) name. These days, in Quebec, a woman legally keeps her own family name, frequently hyphenating it with that of her husband. Even in the eighteenth century, if you have access to actual documents and letters, you will find that French married women usually include their maiden name in their signature. Scottish communities are also inclined to designate married women by their maiden name; a custom all genealogists should encourage and applaud.

Ned and Molly, Ted and Dot

Another hazard can be the nickname that appears as a personal/Christian name. In English, the common short versions, Bill for William, Liz for Elizabeth, or Bob for Robert, are so familiar they can be misleading if they actually derive from some other source. Bert can be short for Albert, Herbert, or Bertram; Ed may be short for Edward, Edmund, Edgar or Edwin. Edward also becomes Ted, or Ned, but Ted may also derive from Theodore, and my cousin Ned's name was Edmund. Polly or Molly are common 18th-century diminutives for Mary; Bell may be Isabel, but might be Belinda. Keep your wits about you and never hesitate to consult dictionaries of names.

In the 1880s there was a fad for giving girls "poetic" names rather than plain old family ones like Jane, Lydia or Mary. That is how my Grandmother came to be "*Althea* ", and her cousins "*Arvilla Lidinia* ", "*Madena* ", and "*Ella Blanche* " (called "Nellie"). Census takers tend to avoid such problems by writing a large capital letter and a squiggle. As for spelling given names like these, we must accept that only friends and family will get it right.

Pride and prejudice

In the 1850s, after the huge influx of famine-driven Irish, many families of Scottish origin insisted on the Mac--- spelling to distinguish themselves from the socially inferior Irish Mc---. My own great-grandmother McCoy tried vainly to change the name the family used to "*Coy* " because a family of that name were prominent early settlers in New Brunswick. As a result I have found documents with McCoy, Mecy, Coy and even Cony on them.

Immigrants from eastern Europe or the Orient present a particular problem, since English-speaking clerks might not have any idea of how a name should be spelt, particularly if the immigrant's passport or documents were in the Greek or Cyrillic alphabets, Arabic, or an Oriental script. Look first for phonetic variants and, again, ask someone who knows how the name would have been pronounced and what it meant. Translation was often the answer to names others could neither spell nor pronounce.

At the end of World War II, Veteran's Benefits put many second- or third-generation Canadians through university. As they moved into the professions, they faced considerable social and economic pressure to make their name "less foreign". If the original name is long, consider how it might be shortened. I once found a sequence of directory entries where a family from central Europe first appeared as *Tatarachuk*, then *Tarchuk*, and finally as *Tarc*. It was clear the family deliberately dropped syllables. Alas, even in the 1950s, there was prejudice against names that ended in "isky" or "chuk". By the early 1960s, most names seem to appear with their European spelling.

Immigrants from cultures where a different name order is used sometimes claim their personal name was written down as a family name; but there is also the common British custom of using a family surname as a personal/Christian name. If, like my husband Creighton Douglas, your Christian name (*Creighton*) was originally a family name, and your family name (*Douglas*) is a common personal name, and, if there is a "*Douglas Creighton*" in the same class at school, you learn to live with the confusion.

USEFUL PUBLISHED SOURCES

Most public libraries have a shelf of books on personal or family names, and many large Dictionaries have a section on "Personal Names", for example:

A Dictionary of Surnames, compilers: Patrick Hanks and Flavia Hodges. Oxford, New York: Oxford University Press, 1988.
> Has entries for most major surnames of European origin (but not all). The same authors and press brought out *A Dictionary of First Names* in 1990; it includes other language groups as well as English.

Chambers 20th-Century Dictionary, editor: E.M. Kirkpatrick.
Edinburgh: W.R. Chambers Ltd., new edition, 1983.
>Has "Some English Personal Names" listings (pp. 1565-1575), including both diminutive and foreign language spellings (including Latin). It also has 22 pages of abbreviations explaining those initials that may follow a name, like J.P., M.L.A., C.B., or K.C.M.G.

Répertoire des noms de famille du Québec des origines à 1825,
by René Jetté et Lécuyer Micheline.
Montreal, QC: Institut généalogique J.L. et associés, 1988.
>A helpful guide through the A--- *dit* B---- maze for Quebec families.

Both the Drouin (113 vols.) and Loiselle (microfiche) marriage indexes cross-reference most Quebec *dit* names, and there is an *Index des surnoms et sobriquets* on microfiche (31 fiches), available at Les Archives nationales du Québec/National Archives of Quebec, and probably elsewhere.

W.J. Douglas' *Diary*, October 1887: note second entry—the baptism of Bessie.

Chapter 7

FAITHS OF OUR FATHERS

Disestablishmentarianism — or merely Canadian?

Methodist records are in the United Church Archives, **Presbyterian** registers may be *there* or with the Presbyterian Archives and, if the family said they were **Episcopalian**, check in both the Church of England and the Methodist-Episcopal records. The Church of England Parish Registers are kept by the individual **Anglican** Diocesan Archives; those of the **Roman Catholic** church are also with their Diocese, but the Diocesan boundaries of the two denominations are different.

Confusing? The nineteenth-century religious denominations you may find on a census return can be more than a little puzzling. Because settlers came here from the United States as well as Great Britain, our religious institutions evolved from both British and American churches and sects. Thus two different branches of the same denomination might be rivals in parts of British North America (now Canada). The result is a tangled web of terminology, difficult for Canadians to understand, and worse for others.

A little theology may be a dangerous thing, but for family historians it is important to know something about how different denominations organize their churches, the lines of authority and, consequently, what their archives may hold. In the Christian Church, there are two basic forms; **hierarchical** and **congregational**. Hierarchical denominations like the Roman Catholic and Anglican (*Episcopalian*) churches, view authority as descending from Heaven to Pope or Crown, thence to Archbishops (Archdiocese), then Bishops (Diocese), and so down to Parishes and individual parish Priests, Rectors, or Vicars.

Such a structure can manage a world-wide organization with many and varied individual sub-structures (such as religious orders that teach or provide for medical or social needs), but is, by its very nature, authoritarian. For family historians their great virtue is the production and preservation of excellent and continuous records — at least where fire, damp, mice and men have not been too active.

Rebels against these established churches tended to form congregational structures, where each congregation is responsible for its own activities but come together with other groups in some sort of co-operative group (**Synod**, **Conference**, or **Council**) to manage affairs that go beyond the smaller unit. They have a tendency to split over minor points of theology and go off in all directions; their history is sprinkled with charismatic preachers and leaders. Their records, alas, are only as good as the individual sect, minister, or congregation, wanted them to be.

The colonies in the New World attracted many settlers because they offered religious freedom; some more, some less. The result is a confusing number of religious denominations that split and change and then merge again at the end of the 19th century. Sorting them out has been done for Canada in the *Historical Atlas of Canada, Volume III*, Plate 34: "Religious Adherence", which uses both multi-colour maps and pie-charts to display the religious diversity across the country. In 1891, a pie-chart shows slightly over 50% of Canadians were **Protestant** (Methodists, Presbyterians, Anglicans, Baptists and Lutheran), over a third **Roman Catholic**, and a very small wedge took in all the "others", including **Jews** and **Quakers**.

Religion and the Census

The data used in the *Atlas* is taken from the relevant Canadian census returns where, unlike those of the United States, a column for "religion" was a standard element. This is very useful for family historians, but some cryptic abbreviated entries may prove difficult unless you know about the many and various denominations and sects.

R.C. is obviously **Roman Catholic**, C. of E. is the **Church of England** (now *Anglican*), though I did find a French-speaking census enumerator who wrote it as "Englican". Fair enough, for, in England, it is the established church, which means rather more than the "church of the establishment", though that is a pretty good definition of its social position. It never had the same power in the British colonies, where freedom of religion had been a factor in attracting non-conformist settlers. Though certain Bishops tried to establish Anglican dominance in Canada, in Quebec, after the conquest, influence was shared with the Roman Catholic Church and, by 1831, all non-conformist clergy had been granted equal rights.

Pres. is **Presbyterian** (a member of a church governed by elders, all of equal rank), a definition that applies to those labelled C. of S. (the **Church of Scotland** or the **Kirk of Scotland**), but not to the Episcopal Church in Scotland. F.C., or P.F.C., is the **Presbyterian Free Church**; R.P. is the **Reformed Presbyterian**; U.P. is **United Presbyterian**. **Cameronians** were a small group that broke from the Church of Scotland, and were active in early Eastern Ontario settlements.

If early Presbyterian congregations were schism-prone, so were their **Methodist** neighbours, who may appear as M. or Meth. or as Wes., W.M., or **Wesleyans**. E.M. means **Episcopal Methodists**. **Baptists** are usually shown as Bp. or Bap.; **Quakers** as Q; **Universalists**, **Bible Christians** (B.C.), and other less familiar sects, are generally written out. Every now and then some individualist says "None". [1]

In the *Historic Atlas:* Plate 34, G.J. Matthews has drawn a pedigree chart illustrating "The Road to Church Union". It shows clearly how many local and regional Presbyterian Synods had to join together to form the Presbyterian Church in Canada (1867), and is equally enlightening as to when and how Wesleyan Methodists, Methodist Episcopal Churches (USA and Canadian), Primitive Methodists, Bible Christians and New Connexion Methodists slowly got together as the Methodist Church of Canada, Newfoundland & Bermuda in 1884.

The United Church of Canada

The United Church of Canada is an institution unique to this country that researchers from other places may not be familiar with. On 10 June 1925, **Church Union** amalgamated the **Methodist Church of Canada**, about half the **Presbyterians**, the **Congregational Union**, and the **Union Churches**

---

[1]   See: *Catalogue of Census Returns on Microfilm ... 1666-1891* (Ottawa: Public Archives of Canada, 1987). The "Introduction" contains a list of abbreviations, p.xii, along with a concise explanation of the census schedules.

of Western Canada into the United Church of Canada. Since the United Church absorbed all the Methodist and Congregational churches in Canada, it holds whatever earlier records survive from these two groups. However, not all Presbyterians joined so their records are divided between the United Church and the Presbyterian Church of Canada.

Church Archives

Like all things Canadian, church records and those who hold them, are divided regionally, not so much by province as by early church districts. The principal **Archives of the United Church of Canada** are located at *Victoria University*, a part of the University of Toronto, but there are also six regional Conference Archives, and some material is held at various universities, like *Mount Allison* in Sackville, N.B., that were founded originally as denominational colleges. The same holds true for the Baptists. **The Canadian Baptist Archives** are at *McMaster Divinity College* in Hamilton, Ontario, but *Acadia University Archives* in Wolfville, N.S. holds the historic records of the Baptist Church in Atlantic Canada.

The *Directory of Canadian Archives* lists most church and denominational archives and gives some idea of their holdings. There are addresses for the various Anglican Diocese archives, Roman Catholic Archdiocese, Diocese, and some parochial archives, as well as those of many Roman Catholic Religious Orders.

The **Lutheran** and **Mennonite** Church's archives are also included, and the **Salvation Army** and the **Canadian Jewish Congress National Archives**, but there is nothing to tell you that the **Society of Friends** (*Quakers*) holdings are at *Pickering College* in Newmarket, Ontario, much less that they are extensive and available on microfilm at the Archives of Ontario and the National Archives of Canada.

USEFUL PUBLISHED SOURCES

The Ontario Genealogical Society will publish a *Guide to Research in the The United Church of Canada Archives*, being prepared by the Archivist at the UCC Archives and available in 1996.

Directory of Canadian Archives,
Ottawa: Canadian Council of Archives, 1990.
> There should be a new edition soon after this booklet is published. For the addresses of Religious Archives look in the index that groups archives by category, under "Religion".

The Encyclopedia of Canada, general editor, W. Stewart Wallace.
Toronto: University Associates of Canada, 6 vols., 1935-37;
registered ed. 1940; 2nd ed. 1948.
> Contains useful brief histories of the major Christian denominations and many individual Religious Orders (look under "Sisters", "Brothers", Jesuits etc.).

Archivaria, No. 30 (Summer 1990). Journal of the Association of Canadian Archivists, published semi-annually.
> No. 30 is devoted largely to Canadian Religious Archives, and between the various articles, "Notes and Communications" and the book reviews, provides an overview of less well-known archival activities; for example, a description of the project that produced the *Guide to the Records of the Canadian Unitarian and Universalist Churches, Fellowships, and Other Related Organizations,* comp. Heather M. Watts, (Halifax, N.S. 1990).

Archivaria, No.31 (Winter 1990-91),
> Describes "Menonite Archives in Canada" and you will also find a review of *Records of the Anglican Church of Canada. Volume 2: Guide to the Holdings of the Ecclesiastical Province of Ontario.* A joint effort of the archivists of this ecclesiastical administrative unit, it is the second volume in a series that originated in 1986 with *Guide to the Holdings of the Archives of Rupert's Land* (remember Rupert's Land? the name survives here). Guides for the two remaining Canadian ecclesiastical provinces are in preparation.

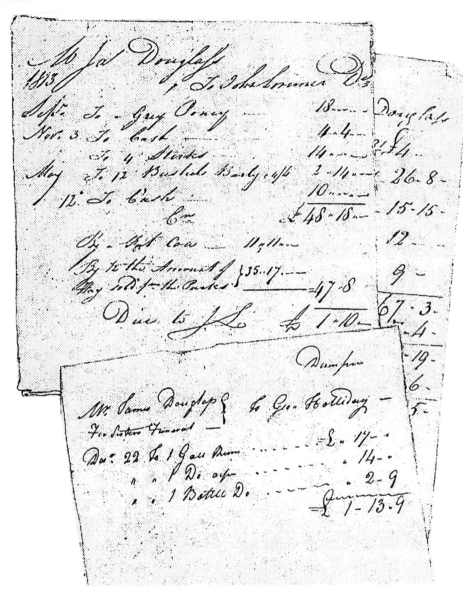

Family accounts show how, in Scotland, a "Fat Cow" could be part payment for a "Grey Poney" and four young cattle, but that a gallon of rhum for a funeral wake required cash. Such barter was even more common in North America, though most publicans were equally cautious in requiring cash.

Chapter 8

COIN OF THE REALM

Will you be paying in Halifax currency or York?

> "Our currency is now like a Scotch haggis, made up of contradictions, of things good and bad ..."
>
> *Acadian Recorder,* 21 October, 1820

The money that circulated in the North American colonies was, to say the least, varied. **Sterling** was the official currency in British colonies and tax assessments and valuations are normally given in **pounds, shillings** and **pence**. Little sterling currency circulated, however, and the Spanish "**Dollar**" was used widely throughout the Americas. To refresh your memory, here is a table from the back of an old scribbler that predates the decimal conversion (1968 to 15 February 1971), perhaps you can date the scribbler from the exchange rates in the right-hand column:

ENGLISH MONEY TABLE

4 Farthings	= 1 Penny (d.)	A Florin is 2s.	= 45¢
12 Pence	= 1 Shilling (s.)	A Half Crown is 2s. 6d.	= 60¢
20 Shillings	= 1 Pound (£)	A Sovereign is 20s.	= $4.86

Pre-decimal Sterling is typically written as: £2-13-7 or £2/13/7
14s 4d or 14/4

The guinea, at one time a gold coin worth 21 shillings, was coined by Britain for the African trade. It remained as a money of account (for calculating professional fees and pricing luxury goods).

In North American documents and deeds of sale, there may be references to "**provincial currency**", "**Halifax currency**" or "**York currency**". These are also monies of account for which no coinage or bills ever existed. Their values were fixed by government decree. A curious example of a money of account was the Hudson's Bay Company's "**made beaver**", equal to the value of a prime male beaver pelt. As a commodity, of course, the value was variable, but the Company eventually (in 1854) issued a token of this value.

Here be Dragons!

In New France, the legal silver **écu** and the illicit Spanish silver "**dollar**" both circulated, together with "**Card Money**", an informal but officially signed-and-sealed form of paper money. In Massachusetts and Nova Scotia, the Spanish silver dollar was rated at 5s., but in the New York colony it was rated at 7s. 6d. and, a little later, at 8s. Thus there was available two monies of account, introduced by merchants from these colonies: **Halifax currency** used the 5s. rating, while **York currency** used the New York valuation.

Five weeks after the fall of Quebec in 1759, the French Government repudiated the obligations represented by the card money, eventually redeeming most of it at about 25% of face value. This gave "**paper money**" a bad reputation for many years. The British administration tried to resolve the Halifax and York currencies confusion and, in 1764, passed an ordinance establishing official ratings in British currency of all coins circulating. The Spanish dollar was given a value of 6s. but during the American Revolution this was reduced to 5s., making Halifax currency the standard. However, York currency valuation was still widely used in Montreal and Upper Canada.

Coins in circulation came from all over the world. Small denominations were in especially short supply and Provinces, banks, manufacturers and merchants issued their own coins and tokens. Settlers welcomed any specie (coin money) they could lay their hands on.

In 1785, the new United States formally retained the dollar as the standard unit of currency with decimal subdivisions. The first true American dollar was minted in 1794, but Spanish dollars continued in use and remained legal tender until 1857. The adoption of decimal coinage by the United States caused much of its older silver to come to Canada where it was over-valued but a welcome addition.

In the colonies that remained British, the official shift from Sterling to decimal (dollar) was gradual. The *Provinces of Canada Currency Act of 1853* legalized transactions in decimal currency for the first time. Gold coin was made unlimited legal tender, and the adoption of the Gold Standard dates from this time and continued until 1914. On 1 January 1858, an Act came into force requiring that accounts of the Province of Canada be kept in dollars and cents. By the middle of the year, the first shipment of Canadian coins was received from the British mint. The *Uniform Currency Act of 1871* extended the decimal system to Nova Scotia and, in 1881, the scope of the act was extended to include Prince Edward Island and British Columbia.

USEFUL PUBLISHED SOURCES

Money and Exchange in Canada to 1900, by Alan McCullough.
Toronto: Dundurn Press, 1984.
> The definitive source, with many tables of official ratings and equivalent values over the years.

The Encyclopedia of Canada, general editor: W. Stewart Wallace. 6 vols.
Toronto: University Associates of Canada, 1935-37;
registered edition, 1940; 2nd edition, 1948.
> The "Currency" entry explains the whole tangled web in some detail.

The Story of Canada's Currency,
s.l.: printed for the Bank of Canada, third edition, 1981.
> Gives a simpler but more entertaining account in its 38 pages.

History of Canada Currency and Banking, 1600-1880, by Adam Shortt.
Toronto: Canadian Bankers' Association, 1986.
> Reprint in facsimile from *The Journal of the Canadian Bankers' Association* issues Apr, Jul, Oct, 1898; Jan & Apr, 1899.

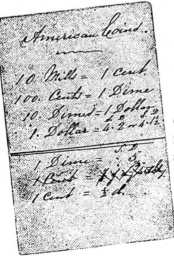

Converting decimal money to the familiar Sterling values confused some settlers.

Passengers' Contract Ticket for James Douglas & family, June 1850.

Chapter 9

LOYAL BRITISH SUBJECTS and PASSENGER LISTS

Only aliens must be naturalized.

On 1 January 1947, the **Canadian Citizenship Act** came into force.

Before that date, people born in British North America or, after 1867, in Canada, were all "*natural-born British subjects* ". Immigrants from Great Britain and the Commonwealth, who were also British subjects, were automatically considered citizens, with the rights and responsibilities that that brought. Only aliens had to be naturalized, and Americans were "aliens".

Records of immigration to British North America are sparse compared to the United States. The main reason is that the majority of those who arrived by sea were already British subjects. Few records were kept of this essentially internal migration, unless the individuals were part of some special subsidized group or settlement plan.

Oath of Allegiance

In the colonies, a person normally had to swear an oath of allegiance if they obtained a grant of Crown land. So did anyone taking public office. Quakers and others, whose religion forbade an oath, made an affirmation.

In the 1820s and 30s, it was American aliens crossing the border in search of land who worried the government of Upper Canada. Would they become loyal subjects of the Crown, or a subversive fifth-column—to use a 20th-century term—if the Americans invaded again. Regulations against such aliens owning land had proved unenforceable. Finally, in 1828, the Upper Canada Legislature passed **An Act to Secure and Confer Upon Certain Inhabitants of this Province the Civil and Political Rights of Natural Born British Subjects**.

Aliens who had lived in the Province for seven years were expected to take an oath of allegiance (or affirm allegiance) within three years. Registers were kept of everyone taking the oath and these *Upper Canadian Naturalization Records* have been published.

For more recent records of naturalization, their destruction, and the restrictions imposed by Privacy legislation, consult *Tracing Your Ancestors in Canada*, available free from the National Archives of Canada.

Passenger Lists

In Great Britain, keeping a record of emigrants was attempted during a few brief periods. Those kept between 1773-1776 include sailings to Nova Scotia and are published in Fothergill's *Emigrants From England 1773-1776*. The British Colonial Office correspondence files (ser. 384) contain some lists of assisted emigration, mostly from Ireland (Index 1817-1831, NAC mf. C-4252). Passenger lists are equally sparse. The *Genealogist's Handbook for Atlantic Canada* lists a few passenger lists and manifests for the Port of Saint John, New Brunswick, for 1833-34 and 1837-38; some seventy lists at the Provincial Archives of Nova Scotia; a few more for Prince Edward Island, plus a handful of reconstructions for Newfoundland. Reconstructions using various documentary sources are being developed for the French colony of Quebec, but for the masses of settlers who poured into the ports of Quebec City and Montreal in the 1830s to 1860s, to spread westward, there are practically no passenger lists until 1865.

Microfilmed Passenger Manifests

In that year, 1865, the government of the day started to keep passenger manifests of the ships arriving at Quebec City and, in later years, those for other ports. Unfortunately, once these lists were microfilmed, sometime in 1950-1965, the originals were destroyed, thus, unreadable microfilms (and some are) can not be checked against the original. The National Archives of Canada (NAC) has microfilm copies of passenger manifests for ships arriving at certain Canadian ports for these years:

Quebec City, Que.	1865-1919
Halifax, N.S.	1880-1919
Saint John, N.B.	1900-1918
North Sydney, N.S.	1906-1919
Vancouver, B.C.	1905-1919
Victoria, B.C.	1905-1919

The Victoria, British Columbia reels include smaller Pacific Coast ports.

The majority of immigrants from Europe and the British Isles arrived at Quebec City or Halifax. More ships arrived at Quebec than Halifax, but Halifax was open all year and the ships were larger. Some passengers also landed at Saint John, New Brunswick, but many more went on to New York or Portland, Maine, which had direct train service to Montreal.

The NAC has filmed the lists of passengers destined for Canada who landed at: Boston, Baltimore, New York, Portland, Philadelphia and Rhode Island for the years 1905-1919 or 1921 depending on the port. However, these lists include **ONLY** the passengers who told the Purser (who made out the lists) that they were proceeding directly to Canada. Some did not.

Quid pro quo

It has been calculated that approximately forty percent of the passengers arriving in Canada were bound for the United States. No lists were required for people entering the United States overland from Canada and Mexico until Congress passed the *Immigration Act of 1891*. In addition to excluding those suffering from "loathsome or contagious diseases", this Law provided for medical examinations at what became the first United States immigration inspection stations along the Canadian border. In 1909, District 1 of the U.S. Immigration Service was established at Montreal and encompassed the entire Canadian border.

The headquarters were later moved to St Albans, Vermont, where the Immigration and Naturalization Service (RG 85) microfilmed its five series of immigrant records and Soundex indexes covering the period 1895 to 1954. That material is now available as a microfilm publication of the United States National Archives and Records Administration (M1461-M1465, some 1200 rolls of film), and may be accessed through inter-library loan services at local reference libraries or at the LDS Family History Centers.

Using Passenger Manifests

In Ottawa, the National Archives has a guide to the microfilmed manifests that will help you find what port and what years are on what films. There are also lists of arrivals at these ports which give the ship's name and port of embarkation for some years. The order of filming can be confusing but each manifest has an initial sheet giving name of vessel, dates, captain, etc., as well as a summary sheet with name, dates, and totals of passengers in each class (salon, second, steerage, etc.).

The manifests contain much genealogical material: name, age, occupation, intended destination, place of birth, but there are **NO NOMINAL INDEXES**, except for a card-file index of passengers arriving at Quebec City in the years 1865-1869 at the NAC.

Individual Pursers had their own ways of keeping these lists. Country of birth entries are not always geographic; some are ethnic identifications like "Russian German". With British emigrants, under "Country/or County of Birth", some Pursers put down "England", others put down the actual County, some list surname first, some the personal name; some use rubber stamps, some don't. Some (of blessed memory) make their lists alphabetical—most do not.

Passenger Manifest searches are relatively easy, but very slow, since the names are rarely in any order and many thousands of immigrants arrived each year. Unless you have infinite time, leave such searches until you have done as much other family research as possible. It is vital to know the passenger's name at the time of arrival, who accompanied them, and at least the year of arrival. The time of year is better still (a mid-winter arrival eliminates Quebec City). The name of the ship will narrow the search, though most made several crossings in a season. Being certain of the port is equally helpful, but be aware that family tradition is not always accurate, particularly if it has been passed down orally over two or three generations. American naturalization records may contain some of this information.

The **CANADIAN PACIFIC RAILWAY** and the **GRAND TRUNK RAILWAY** (which merged with some other lines to eventually form the **CANADIAN NATIONAL RAILWAY**) served Canadian ports, and had direct lines to Portland, Maine, and New York City. They promoted immigration and provided the primary transportation to inland cities.

European Emigration Records

Some emigration records survived World War II, notably at Hamburg, Germany, and Aalborg, Denmark. Emigrants from many parts of Europe left through the port of Hamburg and, in 1850, the "Hamburg Association for the Protection of Emigrants" was founded. Today, records are indexed, computerized, and staff will deal with your queries in English. If you think your ancestors may have sailed from the port, you can contact:

> Historic Emigration Office
> Museum für Hamburgische Geschichte
> Holstenwall 24
> 2000 Hamburg 36, GERMANY

If you have Danish roots, the address to write is:

> The Danes Worldwide Archives
> Ved Vor Frue Kirke
> P.O. Box 1731
> 9100 Aalborg, DENMARK

USEFUL PUBLISHED SOURCES

Upper Canada Naturalization Records 1828-1850, by Donald A. McKenzie. Toronto: Ontario Genealogical Society, 1991.

Genealogist's Handbook for Atlantic Canada Research,
Editor: Terrence M. Punch, CG(C).
Boston: New England Historic Genealogical Society, 1989.

Emigrants from England, compiler: Gerald Fothergill.
Baltimore: Genealogical Publishing Co., 1964.

A Dictionary of Scottish Emigrants to Canada Before Confederation,
compiler: Donald Whyte, F.H.G., F.S.G.
Toronto: Ontario Genealogical Society, Volume 1: 1986; Volume 2: 1996

Here be Dragons!

The following **INDEXES** are available in many research libraries and may be helpful, particularly if ancestors came through the United States.

Passenger and Immigration Lists Index: a guide to published arrival records of about 500,000 passengers who came to the United States and Canada in the seventeenth, eighteenth, and nineteenth centuries, 3 volumes.
editors: P. William Filby and Mary K. Meyer.
Detroit: Gale Research Co, 1981;
> Annual supplements have been issued since 1982. The plan is to publish annually one supplement of approximately 125,000 names, taken from small passenger lists in journal articles and books as well as the names from very large undertakings such as the seven-volume *Famine Immigrants, 1846-1851.*

Passenger and Immigration Lists Bibliography, 1538-1900, being a guide to published lists of arrivals in the United States and Canada,
compiler: P. William Filby.
Detroit: Gale Research Co., 1981, Supplement, 1984.
> Hundreds of passenger lists not yet included in the above *Passenger and Immigration Lists Index* are cited.

Morton Allan Directory of European Passenger Steamship Arrivals for the years 1890 to 1930 at the Port of New York and/or the years 1904 to 1926 at the Ports of New York, Philadelphia, Boston, and Baltimore.
New York: Immigration Information Bureau, Inc., [c1931].
Baltimore: Genealogical Publishing Co., 1979 reprint of the 1931 edition.
> Occasionally useful, this book contains the "arrivals of passenger steamships carefully compiled by the calendar year and indexed alphabetically by Steamship Line." Remember, some ships stopped at Halifax on their way to U.S. ports. Includes a list of shipping lines that discontinued passenger service to United States ports by 1931.

A Dictionary of Immigrants to Nova Scotia, by Leonary H. Smith.
Clearwater, FL: Owl Books, c1985.

The Famine Immigrants: lists of Irish immigrants ..., 1846-1851, 7 vols.
editors: Ira A. Glazier & Michael Tepper.
Baltimore: Genealogical Publishing, 1983-1986

Chapter 10

THE LOCAL MILITIA AND BRITISH GARRISONS

With some notes on V.I.P.s and Local Government

> **militia** *n.* a military force, esp. one raised from the civil population and supplementing a regular army in an emergency.

> **garrison** *n. & v.* **1.** the troops stationed in a fortress, town, etc. to defend it. **2.** the building occupied by them. *v.tr.* provide (a place) with or occupy as a garrison. **2** place on garrison duty.

> ▸ **garrison town**: a town having a permanent garrison.

In the United States, groups calling themselves **MILITIA** have been making headlines. *Militia* is a term unknown in American military terminology; their part-time soldiers are the National Guard, organized by State. In Canada, where our Militia has a long and honourable history, there is now considerable danger that the term will be misused and misunderstood.

The invasions of 1775-76 and 1812-14 convinced Britain that the United States was a potential aggressor and so the British Army built fortifications at strategic points along the border and vital waterways. Here they maintained small **GARRISONS** of their regular Army. However, through much of the 19th century, the **LOCAL MILITIA** was the mainstay of our defence. Local Militia assisted British regulars to repel the invading Americans in 1812-1814, and served in 1866 and 1870 against the Fenian invasions from the United States. There are land grant documents and medal registers recording such service.

Universal Compulsory Service

Under the *Lower Canada Militia Act of 1803* and the *Upper Canada Militia Act of 1808*, the Militia was composed of all able-bodied men between the ages of 16 and 50 or, 60, in case of national emergency (Quakers, Mennonites and Dunkards, whose religious convictions forbade military service, could be exempted on payment of a fine). The colonies in the Maritimes also maintained this form of universal compulsory service. Units were formed on a local basis, usually by County. The higher ranks of Militia officers were often officers who had retired on half-pay from the British army and taken up land grants in the colonies. Published **MILITIA LISTS**, naming officers only, are quite common in *Almanacs, Directories,* and such.

The county Militias were not a formal "military force"; they supplied their own weapons and turned out once a year for a day of training, usually on the 4th of June, birthday of King George III. Attendance was compulsory at this annual muster of the Militia with a small fine for "delinquency". Later termed the **SEDENTARY MILITIA**, they might be called on in an emergency, either in a general call up *(levée en masse)* or more often in a selective draft by ballot or lot. The period of such service was usually limited to six months.

There are a few nominal **MUSTER ROLLS** at the National Archives, and others exist in provincial Archives. However, on 7th November 1828, the Adjutant General's Department of Upper Canada ordered each regiment of the sedentary militia to submit a nominal roll of the men in their units between the ages of 19 and 39. These are at the National Archives [RG9,1B2, Vols.29-31] and have now been published as *Men of Upper Canada: Militia Nominal Rolls, 1828-1829* (see below). Some 27,000 men are listed, virtually a census of able-bodied males in the province; almost as valuable are the maps of townships and military districts, the tabulation of townships, counties and regiments, and the explanation of how the Militia was organized.

After the defeat of Napoleon, military settlements such as those in **Perth**, **Lanark** and **Richmond** in Upper Canada became part of Britain's answer to the American threat. Here half-pay officers and discharged soldiers were given land in proportion to their rank. They were expected to settle, clear farms, and give the local militia a nucleus of professional soldiers to reinforce the small garrisons of British regulars. **CHELSEA PENSIONERS** (wounded soldiers pensioned out of the army through the Chelsea Hospital, London) were allowed to exchange or commute their pension for a grant of land or money. They were sometimes less successful settlers, but such military groups are well-recorded.

British Garrisons

British regiments served in Canada until the *Treaty of Washington* in 1871 (see *Historical Atlas of Canada, Vol.II*, Plate 24: "British Garrisons to 1871"). In addition to their actual military duties, the British regiments made a large contribution to the colonies, not just by their services as surveyors, engineers, and builders, but to the social and cultural life of the garrison towns and cities where they served. Some married (some did not), and children might be born in several towns as the regiment's posting changed.

You may encounter a "**Town Major**"; he was the chief executive officer (staff officer) in a garrison town or fortress, and sometimes he was an officer who had married and remained behind on half-pay when his regiment left the colony.

19th-century developments

The Crimean War saw many British Army units withdrawn from North America and, in 1855, there was a new *Militia Act* that both improved the organization of the Sedentary Militia and established a new force of active volunteers termed the **ACTIVE MILITIA**. This was a group of civilians, uniformed and armed, who went through a brief period of training every year. By 1867, nearly 34,000 men were enrolled in this Active Militia.

Confederation saw the first federal *Militia Act* passed in 1868. It divided the country into military districts, transformed the Sedentary Militia into a Reserve Militia, and allowed the Active Militia to evolve into the Canadian Army. The British Army and the Royal Navy continued to maintain the defense of Canada until 1871, when they withdrew from all but two bases: the Royal Navy's Dockyard, with a small Army garrison, at Halifax; and a naval base at Esquimalt on the Pacific.

These bases would be handed over to the Canadian Department of Militia and Defence at the beginning of 1906, having been extensively renovated, fully-equipped, and left ready for use. The sad decline that followed is lamented by Thomas H. Raddall in *Halifax: Warden of the North* (Toronto: McClelland and Stewart, 1948), pp. 244-5. The *Encyclopedia of Canada*'s

"Militia" entry is equally scathing about Canada's defence forces before the First World War and in the 1930s. British War Office (Army) and Admiralty (Royal Navy) records are in the Public Record Office in England, but most material relating to Canada is available on microfilm at the National Archives in Ottawa. The Military "C" card file index (also on microfilm) simplifies access to some of the material.

Colonel, J.P. and M.L.A.

Sometimes a family treasures Grandfather Smith's commission, believing their ancestor served in the regular Army, when in fact he was an officer of the county Militia. Family tradition often gets the details wrong but almost always contains a solid grain of truth. Such commissions, for example, do indicate that this ancestor was a man of some standing in the community. Tradition could claim he was an important **M.P.P.** (*Member of the Provincial Parliament*), or **M.L.A.** (*Member of the Legislative Assembly*), while research may show he was a long-serving **J.P.** (*Justice of the Peace*), who won a single election and served one brief term in a short-lived government.

To verify legends about these "V.I.P." ancestors, consult the *Almanacs* that were published annually in many colonies. Most include lists of civil and military officials, clergymen, doctors, notaries, and lawyers within the colony, as well as court terms and many local regulations. There are published lists of members of the provincial legislatures of the Colonies and Provinces, though some may cover pre-1841, 1841-1867, and the post-Confederation period in separate volumes with different editors.

The **JUSTICES OF THE PEACE** were appointed by the Provincial governments and presided at the **COURTS OF QUARTER SESSION**, which were the colonies' basic form of local government. The Courts not only dealt with petty crimes (fishing on the Sabbath), business licences (for taverns or ferries) and civil disputes, but appointed most community officials, from **HOG REEVE** (he rounded up any stray swine that got loose) and **FENCE VIEWER** (he settled neighbours' disputes about fence repairs, etc.) to **OVERSEER OF THE POOR**. Records of these courts from the early 19th century often survive, and by mid-century local newspapers usually printed lists of the appointments made each year.

USEFUL PUBLISHED SOURCES:

The Encyclopedia of Canada, general editor: W. Stewart Wallace. 6 vols.
Toronto: University Associates of Canada, 1935-37;
registered edition, 1940; 2nd edition, 1948.
> See "Militia" entry (v.4: pp.290-294).

Tracing Your Ancestors in Canada, reviser: Janine Roy.
Ottawa: National Archives of Canada, 11th revised edition, 1991.
> "Military and Naval Records" (pp.35-38), provides a concise summary of records available at the NAC, Ottawa,

Officers of the British Forces in Canada During the War of 1812-15,
compiler: L. Homfray Irving, hon. librarian, Canadian Military Institute.
Welland, ON: Welland Tribune Printers, 1908.
> Some data on regular British army, but for the most part lists Upper and Lower Canada Militia Officers compiled from land grants, pay lists, etc. Also lists Naval forces in the Great Lakes.

The Service of British Regiments in Canada and North America: a resume ...,
compiler: Charles Henry Stewart.
Ottawa: Department of National Defence Library, 1962.
> Copies of this typescript document are available in most major research and legislature libraries, including a few in the USA.

British Army Pensioners Abroad, compiler: Norman K. Crowder.
Baltimore: Genealogical Publishing Co., 1995.
> Listed by regiment.

Royal Hospital Chelsea Soldiers' Documents: Manuscript Group (MG)13, War Office (WO) 97, Quick Guide Series: Manuscript Division: Number 1.
Ottawa: National Archives of Canada, n.d.

An Index of Land Claim Certificates of Upper Canada Militiamen Who Served in the War of 1812-1814, compiler: Wilfred R. Lauber.
Toronto: Ontario Genealogical Society, 1995.

Men of Upper Canada: Militia Nominal Rolls, 1828-1829,
compilers: Bruce S. Elliott, Dan Walker & Fawne Stratford-Devai
Toronto: Ontario Genealogical Society, 1995.
> Some 27,000 inhabitants, mostly able-bodied men between the ages
> of 19 and 39, as well as some officers and reservists aged 40 to 60
> years, are recorded in the geographically-based units.

The Regiments and Corps of the Canadian Army,
Ottawa: Department of National Defence, Army Historical Section, 1964.

Glenn T. Wright, former senior archivist in the Government Archives Division,
NAC, has presented a series of papers on Canadian Military Records; many
have been published in the OGS's *Seminar Proceedings* or *Syllabus.*

Legislators and Legislatures of Ontario: a reference guide:
Volume 4, 1984-1991, compiler and editor: Debra Forman.
Toronto: Ontario Legislative Library, Research and Information Services, 1992.

Handbook of Upper Canadian Chronology, by Frederick H. Armstrong.
Toronto: Dundurn Press, revised edition, 1985.
> Lists members of parliament for Upper Canada, 1791-1841, principal
> officials of the Civil Establishment, and certain imperial officials.

Political Appointments and elections in the Province of Canada, 1841-1867,
by Joseph Olivier Côté; Appendix to 2nd edition by N. Omer Côté.
Quebec: St Michel & Darveau, 1st edition, 1860;
Ottawa: G.E. Desbarets, 2nd edition enlarged, 1866;
Ottawa: Lowe-Martin, 2nd edition with appendix, 1918.
> Indexed, and exceptionally reliable.

The Legislative Assembly of Nova Scotia 1758-1983: a biographical directory,
editor and reviser: Shirley B. Elliott.
Halifax: Province of Nova Scotia, 1984.
> Updated and revised version of *The Directory of Members of the
> Legislative Assembly of Nova Scotia, 1758-1958.*

The Canadian Directory of Parliament 1867-1967, editor: James K. Johnson.
Ottawa: Public Archives of Canada, 1968.

Chapter 11

LORDS AND LADIES

Titles Were Once Politically Correct in Canada

> Ten Ladies dancing,
> Eleven Lords a leaping ...
> And a Peer in the Fam-i-ly Tree?

That was what many Victorian and Edwardian family historians hoped to find when they took up the hunt for their ancestors. In North America, then as now, very few people understood much about titles, or their proper usage, but they delighted in them nonetheless. Having the same family name as a **"LORD"** or **"SIR"** would almost inevitably lead to a family tradition of noble descent.

Unsubstantiated myths abound. My relatives recount such tales as: "Felix Cochran married Lady Mary Moran; her family disowned her, and the couple came to Nova Scotia in the eighteenth century", or "James Douglas, who came to Canada East, was the grandson of William Sholto Douglas, a son of the 5th Marquess of Queensbury". But my favourite collection of malapropisms is by "Mr B.E. Duffy, the Historian for Sussex Masonic Lodge at Dorchester [N.B.]" and attributed to another ancestor:

> "Mr. Thomas COCHRAN, farmer by occupation. Came from a very distinguished Scotch family of royal blood. Was the youngest son of Lord Dundonald, a Seat of Nobility and brother of Admiral COCHRAN, a former Admiral who fought in the liberation of Peru and was in supreme command of the North Atlantic Squadron, Halifax. The Admiral also championed many just causes in Parliament at Ottawa ..." [1]

I think the writer meant **SCION OF NOBILITY**, not *"Seat of Nobility "*.

---

[1] From a photocopy of part of a typescript account of "The Cochrane Family", no date or author, sent by a friend who "happened to have it" and knew I was interested in the family. Thus are such tales perpetuated — it is "printed", so it must be true!

There were any number of **SCIONS** (a young member of a family; a descendant of nobility) serving in North America with the British army and navy, and assisting the various peers and royals who came to serve in positions of authority. A grain of truth may lurk in family tradition; there may have been a *scion*. However, while titled families are very easy to verify, their bastards are not.

Peers of the British Isles, their families, and most collateral lines, are well-documented from the 18th century onward. The lineages of most of the noble families of Europe are also readily available in print. **KNIGHTS** and **BARONETS** are all on record, though their families are not quite as easy to track. What is more, there is an exact protocol in the usage of titles that will tell you a lot—that is, if the titles are properly used. Alas, they rarely are.

British Honours and Titles in Canada

Since the Canadian House of Commons adopted the Nickel resolution in 1919, no Canadian Government (except that of R.B. Bennett between 1934-1935) has recommended citizens for honours, **bearing titles**, in the Queen's Honours Lists, but it was not always so. At one time in Canada, British titles were almost standard issue for politicians and people of wealth. Almost every Prime Minister received a **KNIGHTHOOD** or **BARONETCY**: Sir Wilfred Laurier (G.C.M.G.); Sir John A. MacDonald (G.C.B.); Sir Charles Tupper (Bart.) to name three. Similarly, military leaders, such as Sir Arthur Currie, were regularly appointed to one or another of the orders of knighthood, and more than one wealthy financier or industrialist was created a baronet, so we have Sir James Dunn (Bart.) and Sir Harry Oakes (Bart.), for example. Medical men, lawyers, and educators were more likely to be **KNIGHTS BATCHELOR**, which is a knight not belonging to a special order.

Canadian newspaper publishers seemed to prefer being "Press Lords" so angled for **PEERAGES**, but such barons as Lord Beaverbrook (Max Aitken) and Lord Thomson of Fleet (Roy Thomson) left Canada and gained their honours in England, as did Prime Minister R.B. Bennett, created Viscount Bennett of Mickleham on 16 July 1941. When he died, childless, 17 June 1947 the title became extinct.

Peers, Lords and Ladies

Remember, "**LORD**" and "**LADY**" are *not* titles. They are styles of address, like Mr, Mrs, or Dr. Not all men styled "*Lord*" are peers, nor do all sit in the House of Lords. In Great Britain, there are five ranks in the Peerage—in ascending order: **BARON, VISCOUNT, EARL, MARQUESS** (often seen in the French spelling *marquis*), and the **DUKE**. Their wives are, respectively: **BARONESS, VISCOUNTESS, COUNTESS, MARCHIONESS**, and **DUCHESS**. Except for *dukes* and *duchesses*, they are addressed as "*Lord*" and "*Lady*".

In Great Britain, only the actual holder of the peerage sits in the **HOUSE OF LORDS**. By courtesy, the **ELDEST SON** of a duke, marquess or an earl takes his father's secondary title, and *his* eldest son, being in direct line of succession, may also bear junior titles. The **YOUNGER SONS** of dukes and marquesses prefix the style "*Lord*" to their Christian and surnames, and their wives are styled "*Lady*", but the man's Christian name should always be used in such courtesy titles. Such "*Lords*" may be elected to the **HOUSE OF COMMONS**. Daughters of dukes, marquesses, and earls are also entitled to use the prefix "*Lady*" with their Christian name. Younger sons of Earls are "*the Honourable*", as are all children of viscounts and barons.

The assorted pitfalls are clearly explained by Valentine Heywood in *British Titles* (London, 1953). Anyone concerned with how to address a duke, or any other dignitary for that matter, should refer to Howard Measures, *Styles of Address* (Toronto, 1969), or any edition of Gertrude Pringle's *Etiquette in Canada* (Toronto, 1932 & 1949).

Orders of Knighthood and Barts.

BARONETS and **KNIGHTS** are *neither* Peers nor Lords, a fact that escapes a great many North American newspaper editors. Both titles are honours; **BARONETCIES** are inherited, **KNIGHTHOODS** are not. Men with either honour are styled "*Sir*", and to distinguish between them when writing, a baronet may have **Bt.**, or **Bart.**, after his name. Their wives are styled "*Lady Husband's surname*" since most married women take their style of address from their husbands. Thus we refer to Sir Winston Churchill and Lady Churchill, or, if you must use her Christian name, Clementine, Lady Churchill.

Here be Dragons!

Never use Lady Clementine Churchill, for the knighthood is her husband's (he refused higher honours) and her father was neither a duke, marquess nor earl. A woman honoured with **DBE** (*Dame of the Most Excellent Order of the British Empire*) is styled "**DAME**".

Biographical entries for any "*Sir Canadian Politician*" will give the date they were "knighted", or made **K.G.**, **K.C.B.**, **G.C.M.G.**, etc. The clearest and most concise explanation of the "letters-after-the-name" these honours generate is found in *The Genealogists' Encyclopedia*, pp.231-32, but most Dictionaries or Biographical Dictionaries list some under "Abbreviations". Their wives are styled "*Lady Canadian Politician*", the few exceptions being women who hold titles (or courtesy titles) in their own right.

While Canada no longer allows citizens to accept British honours bearing titles, the Order of Canada, as well as a number of Provincial orders, have been created to honour our notables. In addition, there are the many medals and decorations for valour, bravery or service, awarded nationally and internationally. The Chancellery, Office of the Governor General, 1 Sussex Drive, Ottawa, ON, K1A 0A1, has issued a pamphlet explaining how these are to be worn and their order of precedence.

One curious "*title*" that occasionally turns up, usually with some headline like "Peer sells 900 year old Title!", is **LORD (and LADY) OF THE MANOR**. In Britain, for 500 years after the Norman Conquest, the manor, an agricultural estate, was the unit of local government. Its head was the *Lord of the Manor* (literally a landlord, not necessarily a titled person) who held the estate from the king, either directly or through one or more **MESNE LORDS**, and governed through the Manor Court. The power to create new manors was lost by the end of the thirteenth century and, over the ensuing centuries, many have disappeared. So those manors that remain usually do date back to the Middle Ages, and the title goes with the land. Even today, if you buy such a Manor, you become the Lord of that Manor and you and your wife may call yourselves *James and Mary Smith, Lord and Lady of the Manor of Wherever*. Shortened to "*Lord and Lady of Wherever*", it impresses North American tourists no end.

Lady Jane?

When a *Lady Jane* or *Lady Mary Moran* turns up in family tradition, you can assume a title is being misused. If you actually do have the daughter of a duke, marquess or earl in your pedigree, it is easily verified. Many reference libraries have some editions of those "**PEERAGES**" that come out every decade or so; select one closest to the time your *Lady Mary* lived. In most libraries, older editions may be in the stacks, with only current ones on open shelves. There will be a cross-index of family names and titles, and check for her, as well, in the listing of "Married Daughters of Peers". Best of luck!

Burke's *Genealogical and heraldic history of the peerage, baronetage, and knighthood* tries to trace the family lineages for the period 1700 to date, but not all the information in the early editions is accurate. Debrett's concerns itself with the living, omitting the dead except where they are necessary to show present relationships. Edmund Lodge's *Peerage, baronetage, knightage* ... came out under various titles from 1832 until 1919 and, while concerned only with the living, contains useful information on aunts, uncles, cousins, etc., of the peers. Living Baronets and Knights are usually listed in the appropriate editions of the Peerages. My one complaint is that most of the editors are perfect gentlemen and never reveal a woman's birth date.

For **EXTINCT PEERAGES** there are at least two volumes to be checked (see Filby below). Now, researchers first consult "Leeson's Lords" (F.L. Leeson, *Directory of British Peerages* ...), which is a complete listing by title and by surname of all British Peerages created before 1984, current and extinct.

These brief notes do not go into the largely political differences between **ENGLISH**, **IRISH** and **SCOTTISH** pre-union peerages. For a brief summary, see *The Genealogist's Encyclopedia*, chapter 13. This work also touches briefly on rules and usage of European and other titles and honours. **FRENCH** titles are complicated because there are *Pre-Revolutionary*, *Napoleonic*, and *Post-Napoleon* grants, but they are quite well sorted through by Albert Révérand, in a series of variously-titled volumes, that were kept up-to-date for many years in his *Annuaire de la Noblesse*. Other **EUROPEAN** countries are even more involved because of varying borders and rulers, but the *Almanach de Gotha*, 1763-1944, is the standard pre-war reference work while a new multi-volume series, *Genealogisches Handbuch des Adels*, 1951- , is slowly working its way through the entire nobility of Europe.

Reality Check

As for Mr Thomas Cochran, of Taylor Village, Westmorland Co., New Brunswick, was he really the youngest son of Lord Dundonald? Any 19th-century edition of Burke's or Lodge's Peerage will give the full Dundonald lineage and neither Thomas, his two known brothers nor two sisters, all living in New Brunswick, are included.

Most Cochran(e) families in the Maritimes have a tradition of being related to **"The Admiral"**. However, the titled [Dundonald] Cochrane family produced at least three Admirals who served in Atlantic Canada so one must ask "Which Admiral?" Check the *Encyclopaedia Britannica*. ***The*** Admiral is obviously Thomas Cochrane, 10th Earl of Dundonald (1775-1860), eldest son of Archibald, the 9th Earl (1749-1831). He held a seat in the British House of Commons at Westminster (not Ottawa) for almost a decade. Disgraced after a sensational trial involving fraudulent stock speculation, he served in the Chilean and Brazilian Navies (same continent as Peru), but was reinstated Admiral in the British Navy on succeeding to the Earldom. He did command the Atlantic and West Indian Station, and his exploits were regularly reported in the newspapers of the day. Even in Taylor Village, a man named Thomas Cochran would have had to take considerable joshing from his neighbours.

USEFUL PUBLISHED SOURCES

Debrett's Correct Form: social and professional etiquette, precedence and protocol, compiler & editor: Patrick W. Montague-Smith. various editions.
London: Debrett's Peerage, c1970; Headland Books, rev. edition, 1992.

British Titles: the use and misuse of the titles of peers and commoners, with some historical notes by Valentine Heywood. 2nd edition.
London: Adam & Charles Black, c1951, 1953.

Etiquette in Canada: the blue book of social usage, by Gertrude E.S. Pringle.
Toronto: McClelland and Stewart, 1932; revised 2nd edition, 1949.

Styles of Address: a manual of usage in writing and in speech,
3rd revised edition, by Howard Measures.
Toronto: Macmillan Co. of Canada, c1962, 1969 reprint.

The Genealogist's Encyclopedia, by Leslie G. Pine.
New York, Toronto: The Macmillan Co., Collier Books, c1969, 1970.

British Orders and Awards: a description of all orders, decorations, ...,
2nd revised edition. London: Kaye & Ward Ltd., 1968.
> Lists all the awards, honours and medals, with notes on military and other ranks.

The following bibliography provides full titles and dates of many editions of various British Peerages, Knightages, Extinct Peerages etc.:

American & British Genealogy & Heraldry: a selected list of books,
compiler: P. William Filby.
Chicago: American Library Association, 1970; 2nd edition, 1975; 3rd, 1983.
> Look for the latest *1982-1985 Supplement* (Boston: The New England Historic Genealogical Society, 1987). Entries for England, Ireland and Scotland are separate, so check under each country.

Recent works not in the 3rd edition of Filby:

A Directory of British Peerages: from earliest times to the present day,
compilers: Francis L. Leeson and Colin J. Parry.
London: The Society of Genealogists, 1984.

If you wish to know more about Lords of the Manor:

My Ancestors Were Manorial Tenants: How can I find out more about them?
by Peter B. Park.
London: Society of Genealogists, 1990.

The Dictionary of Genealogy: the guide to ancestry research, 4th edition.
by Terrick V.H. FitzHugh.
Sherborne, Dorset, ENG: Alphabooks, 1985.
London: Adam & Charles Black, 1994

View of the Mirimichi River. In the early days of settlement, the highways were the waterways and most of the year you needed a conveyance that would float. NAC - C41755

Chapter 12

SOME THOUGHTS ON GEOGRAPHY — FOR GENEALOGISTS

The past is a foreign country — you need a map!

At a recent gathering of genealogists several people made remarks or asked questions that implied our pioneer ancestors travelled via today's four-lane highways. Had I accused these intelligent, experienced researchers of holding such a belief, they would have been most indignant. Moreover, most of them were old enough to have had some youthful experience with single-lane dirt roads and more primitive vehicles than those we drive today. Nevertheless, their mental picture of our country's geography was obviously conditioned by travel in a car on the Trans-Canada Highway or the 401. They fly to Europe, or Vancouver. Travel by ship or train is no longer their norm.

As younger genealogists come along, how much more difficult will it be for them to visualize a land reached by crossing an ocean in a sailing ship, a crossing that could take many weeks, and where the only overland roads were tracks through the forest, far too narrow for a four-wheel drive "Jeep", sufficient at most for someone on horseback.

Yet there were throughways, and highways, and side roads—as any of the original inhabitants could tell you—it's just that they were wet and so, most of the year, you needed a conveyance that would float. In the early days of settlement, most pioneers followed the water routes; so should the researcher.

Topographical Survey maps

No genealogist should ever work far from a Map; not a modern road map, but preferably one that shows as many of the natural features as possible. A particularly useful set for Canada are the *National Topographical Series* of 1:50,000 (approximately 1.25 inches to a mile) maps, prepared in the 1950s.

Based on Military Surveys of 1909-1917 and an R.C.A.F. Aerial Survey in 1950, these maps show every building, identifying churches, schools, sawmills and cemeteries, every road passable or otherwise, railroads, and quite a few abandoned rail tracks. One-room schools and old farms were still standing then and it is possible to locate things on these maps that have entirely vanished today. In addition, because they show topographical details, it becomes clear why roads and settlements are where they are. A brook in hilly country could power a grist mill; a wide, flat valley bottom probably means rich farmland, though cedar swamps are not unknown. Once you have located the ancestral home, a detailed map of the surrounding area may tell you how your ancestors got there, what they did, and where they looked for a mate.

Water highways

If you think of the Atlantic as the freeway to America, then the Saint Lawrence River and Great Lakes are the main highway into the continent. The Ottawa River is the short-cut alternate route while the Richelieu, Rideau, Trent and Grand rivers can be seen as side roads. You cannot settle on land you cannot get to, so the regions that open up first were those accessible by sea and river. The next generation moved to the edges of the established settlements where civilization, such as it was, was only a half-day's walk or canoe ride away. Their children went further inland wherever rivers and lakes made travel possible. Along the Atlantic seaboard, the coastal schooner was the normal mode of transportation until well after the railways were built.

Roads — such as they were

However, with European settlement came horses and wheels, and these require roads. Some roads, such as Craig's Road (L.C.) and Yonge Street (U.C.), were surveyed and laid out for military purposes, others began as blazed trails through the woods, made by prospecting settlers. These trails were cleared to make winter roads between the small settlements and give an outlet to rivers or lakes, where water transport could move produce to market and bring in necessities. Laying out a road was one thing, clearing and levelling it quite another; keeping it passable was almost impossible in any newly-settled area.

By mid-nineteenth century look for roads, but be suspicious. The roads so optimistically drawn on maps by various Land Companies wanting to sell lots, if they existed at all, often remained stump-filled paths for decades. Even so, it was along those trails that many early settlers came. The lucky few whose land fronted on navigable water could bring more of their possessions with them but, for the majority, travel was by "shank's mare" [1]. What they brought was what they, and perhaps a horse or an ox, could carry through the woods.

With a few exceptions, water was an advantage, while hills and mountains were barriers to travel. Villages that seem quite close to each other by modern roads, might once have been accessed only by a roundabout journey to a pass through the hills. Remember when you are checking baptism and marriage dates among early settlers, that muddy roads were impassable in the spring and late fall. The bride and groom, who perhaps should have been wed in November, could not reach a minister until after freeze-up in January and so the first baby came a little early. The itinerant missionary could only get through to the settlements after the roads dried in the summer, and he might (if you are lucky) baptize an entire family—parents and children of all ages—on this one visit, taking his register back to "head office" in Quebec City or Toronto.

Railroads

The situation changed radically and rapidly with the coming of the Railroads. It was in 1832 that a charter was granted to the Champlain and St Lawrence Railroad Company and, on Thursday, 21 July 1836, the first railway train in Canada pulled two coaches from La Prairie, on the Saint Lawrence opposite Montreal, to St Johns on the Richelieu River. The average speed on that first round trip was 14.5 mph. but it provided a direct link to the Richelieu River, Lake Champlain and the water-route to New York. The Railroad boom had begun.

---

[1] This means "to walk". Such old-time, and now obsolete, catch phrases are explained in *Brewer's Concise Dictionary of Phrase and Fable*, edited by Betty Kirkpatrick (Oxford: Helicon Publishing Ltd., 1992).

As well, once pioneer clearings became prosperous farms, the farmers who had acquired horses and wagons saw to it that there were roads. These are the concession roads that form a grid-work on the topographical maps, joining the farms to the "Corner", the "Corners" to the village, and the villages to the Railway Station so the older children could take a train to the Model School in the nearest centre, or the Academy in the closest large town.

The concession roads explain much about the local social life, but the Railroads are what moved most people around rural Canada from the 1850s to the 1950s. A son or daughter could work quite far from home and commute by train, daily or on week-ends. Thus they met and married people from another township or county, and might settle down in a growing town. When parents retired from the farm, they might move to that same town (where children could care for them) and may be buried there. Railroads, however, also made it possible to "take a body home to the family plot", often over considerable distances. Railroad lines were once marked on every road map, now many have vanished but, in numerous libraries, collections of Railway ephemera may include maps and timetables. Do not overlook the information such documents contain.

USEFUL PUBLISHED SOURCES

Among the best detailed maps for the late 19th century are the series of County Atlases, published in the 1860-90 decades; most are republished in facsimile form. Consult *County Atlases of Canada: a descriptive catalogue* (1970) as well as *County Maps: land ownership maps of Canada in the 19th century* (1976), both published in Ottawa by the National Archives of Canada.

Footpaths to Freeways: The Story of Ontario's Roads,
editors: Sharon Bagnato and John Stragge, Public & Safety Information Br. Toronto: Ministry of Transportation and Communications of Ontario, 1984.

Historical Atlas, Vol.II, Plate 25: "Emergence of a Transportation System, 1837-1852"; Plate 26: "The Railway Age, 1834-1891"; Plate 27: "Linking Canada, 1867-1891" which has two maps showing number of days travel from Ottawa in 1867 & 1891; and *Vol.III.* Plate 53: "The Growth of Road and Air Transport".

Chapter 13

WHAT EVERY SCHOOLCHILD USED TO KNOW

During the first half of this century, the following tables were printed on the back cover of most school exercise books and scribblers, along with the multiplication and addition tables. Pupils were expected to know them all by heart.

NUMERALS

Arabic	Roman
1	I
2	II
3	III
4	IV
5	V
6	VI
7	VII
8	VIII
9	IX
10	X
20	XX
50	L
100	C
500	D
1000	M

SQUARE or LAND MEASURE

144 Sq.Inches .... 1 Sq.Foot
9 Sq.Feet .... 1 Sq.Yard
30¼ Yards .... 1 Pole or Perch
40 Poles .... 1 Rood
4 Roods .... 1 Acre
640 Acres .... 1 Sq.Mile

CUBIC or SOLID MEASURE

1728 Inches .... 1 solid foot
27 Feet .... 1 solid yard
42 Feet .... 1 Ton Shipping
128 Feet .... 1 Cord of Wood

LONG MEASURE

12 Lines .... 1 Inch
4 inches .... 1 Hand
12 Inches .... 1 Foot
3 Feet .... 1 Yard
6 Feet............................ 1 Fathom
5½ Yards .... 1 Rod or Pole
40 Rods .... 1 Furlong
8 Furlongs .... 1 Mile
3 Miles .... 1 League
69½ Miles...................... 1 Degree
1760 Yards .... 1 Mile
5280 Feet .... 1 Mile
6075.81 Feet .... 1 Nautical Mile

AVOIRDUPOIS WEIGHT

16 Drams .... 1 Ounce
16 Ounces .... 1 Pound
14 Pounds .... 1 Stone
25 Pounds .... 1 Quarter Can.
or
28 Pounds .... 1 Quarter Eng.
4 Quarters .... 1 Hundredweight
20 Hundredweight .... 1 Ton
2000 lbs. Can. .... 1 Ton
2240 lbs. Eng. .... 1 Ton

TROY WEIGHT

24 Grains .... 1 Pennyweight
20 Pennyweights .... 1 Ounce
12 Ounces .... 1 Pound

Here be Dragons!

LAND SURVEY MEASURE
7.92 Inches	1 Link
100 Links	1 Chain
1 Chain	66 Feet
10 Sq.Chains	1 Acre

MEASURE of CAPACITY
4 Gills	1 Pint
2 Pints	1 Quart
4 Quarts	1 Gallon
9 Gallons	1 Firkin
36 Gallons	1 Barrel
63 Gallons	1 Hogshead

DRY MEASURE
2 Pints	1 Quart
4 Quarts	1 Gallon
2 Gallons	1 Peck
4 Pecks	1 Bushel
36 Bushels	1 Chaldron

PAPER
24 Sheets	1 Quire
20 Quires	1 Ream

APOTHECARIES' WEIGHT
20 Grains	1 Scruple
3 Scruples	1 Dram
8 Drams	1 Ounce
12 Ounces	1 Pound

CLOTH MEASURE
2¼ Inches	1 Nail
4 Nails	1 Quarter
3 Quarters	1 Flemish Ell
4 Quarters	1 Yard
5 Quarters	1 English Ell
6 Quarters	1 French Ell
37 Inches	1 Scotch Ell

DAYS IN THE MONTH

30 days hath September,
April, June, and November.
February has 28 alone,
And all the rest have 31.
But Leap Year coming once
in four,
February then has one day more.

ABBREVIATIONS

A century ago, when a proper education was based on a knowledge of Latin, school children were far more familiar with Latin terms than adults are today. Expect to encounter **LATIN TERMS** and **ABBREVIATIONS** in documents created in earlier times. Newspapers and business documents often abbreviate dates:

'on the 15th ult.'	(*ultimo*)	a date in the preceding month,
'on the 20th inst.'	(**instant**)	[not Latin] the current month,
'on the 10th prox.'	(*proximo*)	a date in the following month.

Abbreviations for the last four months of the year:

September/septembre (7bre, VII^{ber});   **October/octobre** (8^{ber}, VIII^{bre});

November/novembre (9^{ber}, IX^{bre});   **December/decembre** (10bre, X^{ber});

are based on the Latin names for the seventh to tenth months of the Roman calendar, our ninth to twelfth months. They are more commonly used in French texts (**bre**) than in English records (**ber**) but, in either language, clerks or priests may use either Arabic or Roman numerals.

LIBER, or '*Lib.*', meaning a bound volume, is used to indicate specific register volumes, usually with an identifying letter or number. **RECTO** (front side of a leaf) and **VERSO** (reverse side of a leaf) appear when registers are **FOLIATED**, *i.e.*: each leaf (a single sheet of paper) is numbered with the same number on each side, instead of each having its own page number, which we are more used to seeing today. In the index, the two sides of a leaf will appear as 23r and 23v (*i.e.*: leaf *23 recto* and leaf *23 verso*).

The abbreviation for "**FOR EXAMPLE**", **eg.**, **e.g.**, or **ex. gr.**, comes from the Latin **EXEMPLI GRATIA**, and **i.e.** comes from the Latin **ID EST**, meaning "that is to say". People often incorrectly interchange these terms.

When someone is *fl. ca. 1735*, which means **FLORUIT CIRCA** or "flourished about 1735", this tells us an individual has been named in some record which clearly proves that he/she was **ALIVE** about that date (or dates if you have more than one), but neither birth nor death dates are known. Using **c.** or **ca.** (*circa*), or **abt.** (about) in giving a birth, marriage or death date (*e.g.*: **b ca. 1792**) is the standard method of indicating a date has been calculated from other evidence such as the age given in a census or from a tombstone. (See also **NOTES ON DOCUMENTS**, p. 23)

> *On the 25th ult., Mary Brown, relict of the late William Brown, died of mortification.*

If you read those words in an old obituary notice you might giggle and wonder why Mary was so mortified that she died. A good dictionary will probably give the older meanings, *i.e.*: in a time before antibiotics, some unknown "**INFECTION**" killed Mary Brown, the **RELICT** or surviving spouse (now termed *widow*) of William Brown.

Here be Dragons!

The meanings we give to words can change, and if you find an unfamiliar usage of a word, check a dictionary for *(obs.)* **OBSOLETE** meanings. As well, most large dictionaries will provide definitions of the Latin-based medical terms our ancestors used, but the following are a few of the common causes of death or discomfort you may come across:

ague :	recurring fever & chills — usually malarial infection;
apoplexy :	a stroke;
biliousness :	jaundice, often associated with liver disease;
corruption or	
mortification :	infection;
costiveness :	constipation;
croup :	disease of children, with hoarseness and trouble breathing, sometimes confused with diphtheria;
dropsy :	*oedema* (US: *edema*), swelling or watery fluid collecting in tissues, often caused by kidney or heart disease;
falling sickness :	epilepsy;

fevers:

ship's fever, or	
camp/jail fever :	typhus;
lung fever :	pneumonia;
putrid fever :	diphtheria;
remitting fever :	malaria;
flux :	abnormal discharge from the body;
french pox :	venereal disease;
green sickness :	iron deficiency anemia;
kings evil/scrofula :	tubercular infection of the throat lymph glands;
lumbago/sciatica :	lower back pain or back, hip and leg pain;
palsy :	paralysis;
quinsy :	acute tonsillitis;
summer complaint :	diarrhea, often caused by spoiled food or milk.

If your ancestors had further medical complications, you can consult Elizabeth Briggs': *A Family Historian's Guide to Illness, Disease & Death Certificates* (Winnipeg, MB: Westgrath Publishing, c1993), 111 pages of useful data. Available from the publisher and the Ontario Genealogical Society.

Letter to daughter Jennie which includes a poem of thanks for some hand-knit socks and a reference to the death of Maud, his twenty-five year old horse.

James Douglas, Gentleman, commissioned as an Ensign in the New Brunswick Militia.